Judith Adams

QUEUEING FOR EVEREST

OBERON BOOKS
LONDON

First published in 2000 by Oberon Books Ltd.
(incorporating Absolute Classics)
521 Caledonian Road, London N7 9RH
Tel: 020 7607 3637 / Fax: 020 7607 3629
e-mail: oberon.books@btinternet.com

A catalogue record for this book is available from the British
Library.

ISBN 1 84002 154 3

Cover design: Andrzej Klimowski

Typography: Richard Doust

Back cover photograph: Simon Warner

Printed in Great Britain by Antony Rowe Ltd, Reading.

Acknowledgements

The following participants worked for a week in August 1999 and a week in January 2000 in the Crucible Studio developing ideas for a new play about mountaineering and the human spirit. The aims were to explore an initial idea by Judith Adams and research by Judith and Deborah Paige with actors, a fine artist, a choreographer and a photographer and with students participating. We gratefully acknowledge the creative contribution of climbers and expedition organisers based in Sheffield – climbing centre of Britain – and of students from the University of Sheffield.

The play was commissioned by Sheffield Theatres for performance in the Crucible Studio, March/April 2000.

ARTISTIC TEAM

Judith Adams (initiator/researcher/writer)

Gerard Bell (actor/dramaturg)

Raquel Cassidy (actor/developer)

Sushil Chudasama (actor/developer)

Clare Francis (actor/developer)

Ruth Jones (dancer/choreographer)

Deborah Paige (researcher/director/co-ordinator)

Raad Rawi (actor/developer)

Kit Surrey (fine artist/designer)

Catherine Terris (actor/developer)

Leo Warner (video and computer advisor/photographer)

Simon Warner (photographer/installation artist)

CLIMBERS/MOUNTAINEERS

Steve Bell, Jon Tinker, Simon Lowe, Neil Bentley, Ruth Jenkins, Andy Broom, Tom Richardson, Seb Grieve, Chris Morris, Denise Wilson and Allen Jewhurst.

PUJA ORGANISERS

Carlon and Steve

ALSO THANKS TO:

Photographic Inspiration
Alfred Gregory (photographer on 1952 expedition)

New England Correspondent
Robert Utter (grolla in America)

Private Cuttings Agency
Janet Davidson (kippers for breakfast)

Glaciation advice
Christian Edelstam (hot chocolate on the Aiguille de Chamonix)

Le Gîte des Vagabonds, Chamonix – whose International Mountaineering Team got Judith up her first 90 metre pitch on Mont Blanc. (especially Petr and Christian)

Dominic Shellard and the second and third year drama students at the University of Sheffield. (especially Alan, Adam, Emma, Catherine and Sarah)

Rob McKinney and T. Kalsang Sherpa-Baer

The writer wishes to acknowledge direct contribution to the text from all the above, and to say to them and all climbers past and present: *namas-te.*

'She who knows the male
Yet cleaves to what is female
Becomes like a ravine
Receiving all things under heaven.
And being such a ravine
She knows all the time a power
That she never calls upon in vain.
He who knows the white
Yet clings to the black
Becomes the standard by which
All things are tested.
S/He who knows glory yet cleaves to ignominy
Becomes like a valley that receives into it
All things under heaven'

Tao te ching, passage 28

'O the mind, mind has mountains; cliffs of fall
Frightful. Sheer, no-man-fathomed. Hold them cheap
May who ne'er hung there…'

Gerard Manley Hopkins

'Mountains are not a logical world'

Tom Richardson,
mountaineer and climber

'Tireisias: he who delights in signs.'

Robert Graves, *The Greek Myths*

'What is it you have done to me? My heart is heavy
with a beginning so heavy, I put it off. Where are
you? In what corner of the world shall
I find you again?'

Rainer Maria Rilke

Stupa (Virtual Mountain) Notes

In ascending order:

    Base Camp: earth – yellow – a base with the sacred eye

    Ice Fall: water – blue – a dome

    Valley of Silence: fire – red – a triangle

    Death Zone: wind – green – a dish

    Summit/Cave: space – white – a circle

    The Mountain: is played by Herself

Characters

T. ROBIN TRUMAN (T)
the photographer – man aged c.50

GEORGES LAMBERT
Swiss medical technician – man aged 45-50

DA TENZING
Sherpa guide – man aged c.25

THEA ARTEAGA
New England journalist – woman aged c.25

SOPHIE LAMBERT
English wife and mother – woman aged 45-50

BEASTS

YAK

YETI – Ya-te in Tibetan

GORAKS – Himalayan ravens

SNAKE

SNOW LEOPARD

GHOSTS
in the space

OTHER CLIMBERS ON THE MOUNTAIN
(AUDIENCE)

SHERPAS

NIMA – Da Tenzing's sister

CALVIN – Thea's brother

GEORGE MALLORY

SANDY IRVINE

RUTH MALLORY

HENRIETTE d'ANGEVILLE

TENZING NORGAY

TENZING'S MOTHER
RAYMOND LAMBERT
THEA'S EDITOR
OLD MAN OF THE MOUNTAIN
JEHOVAH
PUNDITS

GHOSTS
in the text

LOUIS DAGUERRE
UTNAPISHTIM THE FARAWAY – seer
GILGAMESH – the hero
ENKIDU – the companion
SIDURI – the whore
NINSUN – mother of Gilgamesh
MILAREPA (TEIRESIAS) – of the sacred cave
KALI and SIVA (HERA and ZEUS) – of the sacred
summit

Queueing for Everest was first performed at the Crucible Theatre (Studio), Sheffield on 16 March – 8 April with the following ensemble cast:

Gerard Bell, Sushil Chudasama, Clare Francis, Raad Rawi, Catherine Terris.

Full creative and development team: see page 5–6

ACT ONE

Scenes from the Mountain

The actors playing THEA, SOPHIE and GEORGES enter with the audience – unremarked. They are not in character. T and DA TENZING are already in the space and are in character.

The audience enters as expedition members and are each presented with a piece of orange string long enough to be tied round neck or wrist (see below).

The acting space is simultaneously the mountain and the hospital environment, invoking:

> *1) T's Darkroom and T's Studio, with a painted backdrop of a mountain summit and modern camera on a tripod.*

> *2) Everest Base Camp with prayer flags of words and pictures, rocks, THEA's wall reaching to the upper level and a sloping surface for jumar-ing. Also: climbing clutter (MALLORY's and modern) – especially oxygen canisters.*

All other props are optional and indicated in the text.

A whodunnit? body shape (based on MALLORY's body) is lying in the space. Around the body shape are a Kodak vestpocket camera, a short length of snapped rope, a red neck pouch containing letters and an unpaid bill for the game of fives from Gamages, a broken watch, a blank compass, a single battered shoe, a glove with fingers and thumb cut out, goggles, a head torch, a rusty penknife and a red scarf.

T is hanging wet prints of mountain shots on the prayer lines. DA TENZING is at base camp arranging his own puja (prayer ceremony) with water and candles around a stupa (Tibetan mountain altar) built of the expedition detritus. As the audience enters he perhaps explains the meaning of the water bowls* to some of them, gives small candles, perhaps asks them to toss handfuls of earth/rice. He ties the pieces of orange string round the necks of some of the audience to demonstrate what they are for: a blessing for the journey.

*Note: used both literally (at the Meal Dance) and symbolically throughout the play: 7 bowls of water representing drinking, washing, flowers, scent, music, food, light. All flowers must be narcissi.

As audience settles candles burn around the space and silence falls.

DA TENZING: I pray to the mountain every day.

> *Light on body outline grows bright, bright white.*

PRIEST'S VOICE: 'In his life he sought after
    whatsoever things are pure, high and eternal.
    At last, in the flower of his perfect manhood, he was lost
                                  to human sight
    between heaven and earth
    on the topmost peak of Mount Everest.'

> *Light on body flashes like a camera taking a photograph.*

T: Beginning at the end:
    A fallen man in self-arrest.
    Who?
    How?
    Why?
    A snapped rope around his waist.
    Who is attached?
    Anyone?

DA TENZING: Every day – I pray to the mountain.

T: You can blow your candles out now.

> *More general lighting: a sunny, hot day.*

    It's been a difficult year for us all.
    The Thaw…

> *Soft sound of an avalanche on the higher slopes.*

DA TENZING: Avalanches.
    Many bodies on the mountain.
    She's angry.

T: And right in the middle of the meltdown we find him, too:
   Mallory. George. Herbert (I think). Leigh.
   Mallory.
   Our white knight, arrested on his quest.
   So many years of day exposure, night blackouts.
   Fading into grey like a photograph in sunlight.
   Ectoplasm in silver of what has been.
   That's how we found him.
   But is it Mallory we want?

He picks up vest pocket camera.

   Or this.
   Hard evidence.
   After all: stuff Romance – this a whodunnit. Not who done
   that (*Gestures to body.*) because we know he dun that to
   himself; but had he dunnit before he dunthat? Dunwhat?
   Got to the top of course. First.
   That's what we want to know:
   Who got there first.
   And they're hopeful – the pundits – a Kodak Vestpocket
   Camera will give the verdict, one way or the other.
   Sole witness.
   Silent witness.
   Is there truth – in silence?

Silence.

DA TENZING: I live well. Work hard. For a *Sharwa* I'm
   sober. My mother's a nun and my father a monk. Two
   brothers. Two sisters. One sister dies. Nima. In our
   language: the sun. Nima. My closest sister. I'm three
   beats behind her, always. She leads me on, keeping up
   with her ways. Bad ways they say, and when she dies
   I become good. Good boy. Good son. Good worker.
   Good yak.

The ghost of NIMA (THEA) appears in orange.

We play in the puddles making figures of clay, and when they shout at us, she runs away – laughing.

NIMA runs away, laughing.

I stand like a lump of mud, like a dumb yak, and get two beatings – hers and mine. When she dies they make a doll to save me being taken too. The spirit of the *Ya-te* comes for twins. She eats them together, *Ya-te.* To keep them together. Maybe She knows best. Maybe I'll be happy when *Ya-te* comes back for me.

T: See – we all live our own stories…

DA TENZING: See, if you squeeze the water out of the mud you make mud people. We sit in puddles…

T: …sitting in the dark pit of our private movie houses…

DA TENZING: …squeezing mud people. If they see us we run away, laughing.
Laughing.

NIMA's laughter echoes.

T: …looking up at the stars – and the dark pit and the stars: us. (*Taps head.*) No one else in there.
Stone blind.
All of us.
A Hollywood of loneliness.
Tapping with our sticks along the paths of our own minds. Reaching out our hand, for…what? Who?
An answer?
But, see, if you change…everything changes.

DA TENZING: Maybe they stay there, baking in the sun.
Maybe they're still there, lying in the sun.
So many mud people.
So many ghosts on the mountain.

T: We change.

DA TENZING smears white sun barrier cream and starts to fiddle with a screwdriver and camping stove.

Backdrop of a mountain summit appears. MOUNTAIN GHOSTS appear.

T: These days we queue for the top like punters at a charity dinner dance, because the Hillary Two-Step is a one at a time affair. Up and down.
Statistically speaking, one in six who step through the Death Zone die.
The other five have another burden: proof.
Because these days don't we see how photographs can lie?
'Take my word for it? – There were witnesses?'
Words lie too, we sigh. And witnesses.
'Trust me – I'm an honest man.'
So?
You could be perjuring yourself and not know, the air's so thin up there.
Maybe we have to look at the problem from the other end, as it were.
Maybe something we leave on the summit, to be found?
So – what might be our own, personal Kilroy Woz Here, our beacon for the future?
In the Alps in 1838 Henriette d'Angeville packs in Chamonix for her journey up Mont Blanc with just this question in mind.

HENRIETTE: (*SOPHIE. Scattering belongings.*) Silk for next to the skin. Wool for absorption of heavy rain or wet snow. Map. *Bon.* Sun hat. Bon. Black feather boa. Black velvet mask. Phial of vinegar. Folding penknife. Thermometer. Telescope. Cucumber cream. Potted quail. Carlsbad plums. A large box of handmade chocolates. *Cafetière.* Eau de Cologne. *Bon.* Looking glass. Champagne. Salmon – smoked.
Ah – The Song of Solomon. (*She waves the book.*)

This – this I will leave on the summit of Paradise.

She takes it to the backdrop of the summit and T sets her up for a portrait.

(*With huge theatricality.*) The westerly sun bursts from behind the clouds and I feel that down below in the valley I have lived my days in exile. That my real country is on that snowy, golden peak I see every morning from my balcony, that crowns the valley like a ghost. I am late for my wedding, for my marriage with the face of Israel…for the delicious hour when I can lie on his summit and be wedded to my beloved, my frozen lover. Oh! When will he come?

T: Smile.

T takes a photograph and the ghost of HENRIETTE gives way to the ghosts of MALLORY (GEORGES) and IRVINE (DA TENZING – still smeared with sun barrier cream).

I don't know what you think.
I think people have a right to risk their lives.
But this was his third expedition and he had a wife and children.
I think – well. I've said.

MALLORY: Tent. Blankets. Ice axe. Knife. Altimeter. Thermos flask. Tea. Swan Vestas – 4 packets. Meat lozenges. Sardines. Nestlé's milk. Petroleum jelly. Six one pound bars Fry's chocolate. Puttees. Rope.

T gives MALLORY the vestpocket camera.

Camera.

MALLORY and IRVINE stare at it.

IRVINE: Where did you get that?

MALLORY: Borrowed.

IRVINE: Film?

MALLORY: Ah… (*He hunts around for the film.*)

IRVINE: (*Fondly.*) You're making such a mess.

> *He helps and finds the bill.*

> Unpaid bills on Everest. What a ramshackly man you are.

MALLORY: Health insurance. If we get in a tight spot, Gamages mounts a rescue or loses (*Squints at bill.*) seventeen shillings and five pence. Foreverest.

IRVINE: (*Reading bill.*) 'Five glove. Five balls.' Eton Fives!

> *He drops the bill, T picks it up and pockets it.*

MALLORY: Winchester, old boy.
'One should never be too busy to play fives.'
Old school motto.

IRVINE: (*Taking the camera.*) As far as I can tell there seems to be a film in there already.

MALLORY: Of course. What do you take me for?

IRVINE: What do you take me for?

MALLORY: My dear Irvine: aesthetic pleasure – what else? And your talent with infernal gadgets.

> *IRVINE (DA TENZING) returns to fixing an old oxygen cylinder. T takes the camera from him as he passes and pockets it. MALLORY settles down to writing a letter.*

T: King and Country called. He went. To the trenches with a bad ankle and a murmur of the heart.

> *Sound of trench bombardment.*

> Then to the Himalaya, with same.

> *Sound of avalanche.*

> One battleground for another.

MALLORY: (*Writing.*) 'Dearest – I would have liked to undertake a few other ascents, less ambitious, and perhaps more delightful. But for my part, I'm content enough to have a last crack at Everest. Of the pull the other way, I needn't tell you.

Ghost of RUTH (THEA) appears.

'If I picture the blue Mediterranean and the crisp foam hurrying by as the ship speeds on to Marseille or Gibraltar, I see you smiling in the sunshine on the quayside. My dear one, when such pictures fill my mind, I'm drawn clean out of this tent into a world not only more lovely, more beautifully lit, but signifying…
…something.'

T: Smile.

They do. The picture is taken.

No day-to-day. Just drama-to-drama. And letters. A letter love-affair: Dream of Narcissus. What makes you want to be with a person most? The fear it may not happen? The fear it might?

RUTH: You must go darling.

MALLORY: Are you sure?

RUTH: Yes.

MALLORY: Yes?

He uses handkerchief to wipe a tear from RUTH's eye.

Will you be strong? I'll be strong.

He begins to play with handkerchief.

RUTH: I'll just be here. You have to go, George. I know you. You wouldn't be you if you didn't.

MALLORY: Like war…

RUTH: Yes.

She weeps.

MALLORY: (*Playing with handkerchief.*) Yes.

Long pause as he plays.

You're sure then.

He doesn't look at her. Long pause as he plays.

It looks like this.

He presents a handkerchief version of Everest to RUTH. They both laugh. T photographs them laughing. RUTH retreats.

T: He leaves, loving his wife. She holds him in her heart forever.
Successful marriage is a plan to live alone, together.

IRVINE: My first set of Meccano came from Gamages.

MALLORY: The Empire blesses Gamages.

IRVINE: What will you leave at the top Mr Mallory?

MALLORY: A photograph of my wife. You, Mr Irvine?

IRVINE: (*At a loss.*) My spanner?

MALLORY: And if the tanks fail on descent, dear boy?

IRVINE: Then – dear boy –
We fly.

T takes their pictures in front of the back drop. MALLORY disappears. IRVINE becomes DA TENZING as before.

T BEGINS to bury the body outline with rocks during this speech.

T: Severe frostbite bleaches skin whiter than the snow it dies on.
Unless you get back to sea level, when it sloughs off in black flakes.

He never got down.

Frozen to his mountain.

They chip at him for DNA and frisk his pockets for the camera.

It isn't there.

Neither's he any more – they take a photograph and bury him with rocks.

Twice.

Bury a perfectly good *tableau vivant* and *memento mori* in a late access of tact.

Save us a view of his head on the box – and in the books – and on the website. Oh yes.

Headless on Everest.

Not the stuff of romance you see: a skull, exposed to the sky.

Goraks pecked a hole to his brain. Here. By the time the weather cut through his tweed to the rest of him, his body had – immortalised. Very satisfactory at the slide shows.

Galahad of Everest.

Well done George. Even in your agonising solo death you did your best for us: everything below the neck died aesthetically, with the ineffable grace of a Grecian dancer.

You die – that we might be obsessional.

Ghost of RUTH assumes mourning.

First she hears of it is a reporter on her doorstep.

Even nothing changes.

Flurry of press/flash cameras.

THE PRESS: Mrs. Mallory – do you think they made it to the top before they died?

THE PRESS: When we last saw them they were climbing into cloud.

THE PRESS: Do you have a photograph of the two of you together?

THE PRESS: How do you feel about being left alone…

THE PRESS: …with the children?

THE PRESS: Did he have the right – three times – with children – what's your feeling on this, Mrs Mallory?

THE PRESS: What exactly was his relationship with Irvine, Mrs Mallory; any thoughts?

THE PRESS: After all – Odell was the better bet.

THE PRESS: How does it feel…?

THE PRESS: …knowing you can never bury him?

THE PRESS: …that you'll never see him again – not even the corpse?

THE PRESS: How will you remember him?

T: One minute you live as though a channel's open to another always, and the next, the arteries are torn out and hang bleeding and the world is outer darkness.
Pity.
Ruth.
Penurious Ruth. Alone amid the alien corn of death and fame. And media rapacity.
He once suggested she earn money for the children painting porcelain.

RUTH, distraught, lays a piece of porcelain on the cairn, on which is painted a golden sun and a gold bird flying towards it (as in eagle/sun). Then she disappears.

Silvered like Galahad. Camouflaged like the snow leopard. Bleached by light right out the picture, he climbed on, over the snowfields of our hero worship, seventy years. Questing for our Holy Grail. Self-arrested.

That's what we send them for – our heroes – the Holy
Grail. And no-one, no one, seems to know what's in the
bugger, it should be so desirable. And no-one who might
know what's in it, comes back to us to say.
George?
Is it really you?
Or a mummery? A herring drawn across the trail?
Find you, looking for Irvine.
Irvine's blond you see – at first they say it's Irvine.
Sandy Irvine.
Shy, eager, fair young man from Shrewsbury.
A martyr to sunburn.

He lifts tattered end of rope.

Is it him, or you, or neither? Did he cut this, or you?
Were you above, or Sandy? Who slipped? Who fell? Was
it cut at all? Or did it just wear out?
And never mind the fall – forget the exposure – did you
make the grade?

*He heaps the objects on the stones and adds the MALLORY
clutter.*

This is all you are now – and a scrape of DNA under
glass in a private lab somewhere.
Unless – you left a message on the mountain.

He considers this.

Hillary left his mark on the summit. We know. He told
us. Drank so much, he took a piss.
First man to expose himself voluntarily at such an altitude.
That took some courage.
His partner, Sherpa Tenzing Norgay…

*Ghost of TENZING (DA TENZING) appears and crouches
by the memorial, places on it a photo of Raymond Lambert,
picks up the red scarf, kisses it and wraps it round his neck.*

…climbed with the Swiss the year before, and turned round on the last ridge. His friend was Swiss. Tenzing had to go with the English next year, or miss his chance to be the first. Unless of course, Mallory was the first. And purists might ask: does it count either way, using bottled oxygen?

GHOST OF TENZING: When things go well the Swiss say *Ça va bien*, and when they don't: *Ça va bien*, just the same.
(*French pronunciation.*) *Lambert*…my friend. Forgive me.
I take you with me in my heart.
I take your scarf with me to the summit. I will leave it there.

THE PRESS: Tell us Mr. Tenzing –
Who got there first?
You or Mr. Hillary?
Who got there first?
(If at all).
Who got there first?

GHOST OF TENZING: We reach the summit together.

THE PRESS: Who got there first?

GHOST OF TENZING: We reach the summit almost together.

THE PRESS: What does that mean? Who got there first?

GHOST OF TENZING: There is no sense in such a question. Mountaineers…

THE PRESS: Who got there first?

GHOST OF TENZING: …understand. Please –

THE PRESS: Who got there first?

GHOST OF TENZING: Two men on the same rope…

THE PRESS: What have you got to hide?

GHOST OF TENZING: …are together, in a way…

THE PRESS: What have you got to gain?

GHOST OF TENZING: …together in a way you cannot understand.

THE PRESS: What have you got to lose?

GHOST OF TENZING: Together – alone. Together – and that's all there is to it.

THE PRESS: Who got there first? Who got there first? Who got there first?

GHOST OF TENZING: (*Shouting.*) The answer means nothing. It's the question of fools.

Pause. Silence.

T: (*Gently.*) Would you care to make a statement now, Mr Tenzing?

GHOST OF TENZING: Only that you cannot understand us. Only that you don't know how it feels. You have to be there.

THE PRESS: Smile.

DA TENZING hides his face in the scarf as flash cameras go off. The PRESS retire. DA TENZING removes the scarf.

In telling this story, DA TENZING plays both the following parts.

DA TENZING: My father meets Tenzing Norgay. Not once but twice. When he's a boy – my father – in Solu – he remembers seeing him come down from Chomolungma like a god. He passes through the village to visit his mother, like a god – his feet stride just above the ground, like Siva's. He wears a cap like this. At first they try to pull it off him. He smiles and they stop touching him. Like a god. They cry: '*Shri Tenzing. Zindabar! Shri Tenzing. Zindabar*!' – Lord Tenzing! Great you are! – and throw rice and dance. He passes through to his mother's house, but he speaks with my father. My father is only ten – but he is already bald, as a monk should be, and in yellow robes. He says – *Shri Tenzing*: on the summit, do you see Siva?

GHOST OF TENZING: I see him, yes, holy one – with this, my third eye. (*Head torch?*)

DA TENZING: 'Lord Tenzing, what do you say to him?'

GHOST OF TENZING: I say, *Thuji chey*, Lord Siva: I am grateful. Tell the mother goddess of the snows, tell Chomolungma all will be well now for her and me. Tell her: *Thuji chey*: I am grateful.

DA TENZING: 'Lord Tenzing, how do you climb so high above the earth?'

GHOST OF TENZING: Using these, my four lungs. (*Oxygen cylinders?*)

DA TENZING: He laughs, hitting his chest. 'And what do you do there?'

GHOST OF TENZING: Smile – with my two mouths.

DA TENZING: That is what he says. No-one knows what he means, but this is what he says. My father tells me: 'With my two mouths – I smile'.

Ghost of TENZING'S MOTHER appears. He passes through to his mother's house.

GHOST OF TENZING'S MOTHER: (*SOPHIE.*) So many times I ask you not to go to this mountain.

GHOST OF TENZING: Now I don't have to go again.

GHOST OF TENZING'S MOTHER: At the top, my son –
what do you see?

DA TENZING: (*Aside.*) All her life she believes there's a
golden sparrow on the top of Everest. Also – a small lion
made of living lapis lazuli, with a golden mane.

GHOST OF TENZING'S MOTHER: Did you see the
beasts, my son, as I told you?

GHOST OF TENZING: Yes, mother.

GHOST OF TENZING'S MOTHER: (*To the whole world.*)
Proof!
(*Whispering.*) Did you see Siva, my son? Or Kali?

DA TENZING doesn't reply.

Namas-te! I salute you.

DA TENZING: On the summit he left gifts in a little scoop
in the snow: chocolate, biscuits and lollies. As a child
I dream of standing on the summit of Chomolungma,
scratching in the snow, finding chocolate and lollies and
biscuits, and laughing and hearing my laughter echo
around all the white valleys of the world.
My father says I dream this dream because of my name:
Da Tenzing.

*T takes the letter MALLORY was writing and papers that
have scattered out of the pouch and hangs them on the lines,
like prayer flags.*

All the ghosts gather.

T: Words and pictures.
Ink and paper. Silver and light.
I know which I prefer.
Quicksilver's Mercury.
Messenger between the gods.
You remember those experiments at school when the
mercury escaped onto the inky desk; separated, touched,

combined, rolled apart? Careful, the teacher said, it's
poisonous. I shut him out. Mercury – spoke to me.
See, if you change – everything changes.
Even change itself.
And when change itself changes…
I don't know.
Quick –
Silver.
Silver's our most precious metal, I think.
Gold only reflects the sun. Silver – changes it.
A dark room is a place of alchemy.
Did you never see a face in the developing tray moving
toward you out of the liquid like a ghost?

The Mercury Dance

*Dance of ghosts becoming GEORGES, THEA and SOPHIE. T and
DA TENZING are at the centre of the movement.*

*The following dialogue overlaps, each character carrying on with
their own speech after 'if you…'*

T: See: if you…

DA TENZING: See: if you…

GEORGES: See: if you…

THEA: See: if you…

SOPHIE: See: if you…

T: …change, everything changes.
    What is bird death?
    Turning into a fish now…
    I'm amused.
    How far now?

Pause.

I'm just looking at this.
There. Look.
D'you see? See?
There.
Look. Look.
Gone.
That's incredible.
I'm looking at this now.

THEA: …think about it, try to share too much, it all gets confused. Just do it. It's all a matter of commitment. Committing. I soon learn by falling off that if you don't commit, you don't get very far on a difficult traverse. You can't find the path if you don't let your body look for it. As for mistakes – what's wrong with them? It's faults we use to climb a line.

SOPHIE: …dream ahead there's two possibilities. What happens is always a disappointment. What happens is not as bad as you thought. And dreaming in your head – you can journey again and again. Tidy up the map. My own process.
Is that better than going on a real journey? Or worse?

GEORGES: …work out every day, you hold on to the body of your youth. I gauge myself every year on the mountains. The Alps. The Himalaya. Only a fit man can climb over a certain height without the use of oxygen and still know his own mind. If I descend alive – I descend into the denser air like a god, flying: drunk on nothing more than oxygen.

DA TENZING: …squeeze the water out of the mud you make mud people. We sit in puddles. If they see us we run away, laughing. Maybe they stay there, baking in the sun. Maybe they're still there, lying in the sun.
So many mud people.
So many ghosts on the mountain.

Base Camp

Stupa stage 1: earth/yellow.

DA TENZING begins moving loads over the Ice Fall to Camp One. THEA is sizing up an ice serac in orange outdoor (sexy) climbing gear, carrying crampons and ice axe. GEORGES and T are packing. SOPHIE is waiting. She has a capacious red shoulder bag. ('Red: the colour of heroines in the battle between life and death' – ed.)

T: Two things –
    First:
    I hate linear.
    Fucking hate it.
    Living on a sphere – how can things travel in straight
    lines?
    Living on a sphere – axes spin.
    What is lying may be climbing.
    To climb may be to lie. And time?
    Depends where we are.
    Timeless as snowflakes interlocking.
    Swift as avalanches.

GEORGES: I find packing difficult.
    It's the most difficult activity for me.
    Takes me back somewhere painful.
    I think of all the people I've left behind me and I cry.
    I cry easily – for a man.
    But when it's done…

    He shoulders rucksack.

    …I'm happy.
    Off to new places. New lives.
    After parting – meeting.
    A new journey.

    He sets off for Base Camp.

T: Right.
    Base Camp.

27

Oh – two things I said.
What's the other?
Me.
I'm a fish.
Maybe – a cold fish.
I don't know.
This isn't my story.

T goes to help DA TENZING on the ice fall.

SOPHIE: Alone. Alonement. Aloneness.
An illness.
All my own.
Never to be taken from me.
Not too bad. So far.
I'm being monitored.
How are you, Sophie?
Don't know how. Know where:
I'm at a crossroads.
Without a map.
No-one to talk to about it but me.
How could anyone else imagine it anyway? Every day
I look back on how bad yesterday was and forward over
how bad tomorrow's likely to be – and I don't believe it
myself.
So what could I say?

She writes an imaginary postcard.

'Dear Georges:
I am so alone.
Yours
Sophie.'

She extracts a paper bag from her shoulder bag.

I use a paper bag.
It's a trick they showed me in cognitive therapy.
Or is it yoga?

I panic in a lot of situations.
Especially when they tell me to relax.

She breathes into the paper bag.

Carbon dioxide calms the fight/flight syndrome. They
explained it.
My body's screaming at me: 'Get out of here, Sophie.
Sophie – get out.'
My mind, however, stays put in the process.
Don't you just hate that word? Process. He uses it a lot.
Sometimes I think I'm fine. I walk downstairs to make a
cup of tea. Then I find I'm leaning on the wall, crying.
Tears bouncing off my hands like boulders. Tears no-one
else sees.
And snot.
My actual dreams – at night – are weirdly pleasant.
Which makes no sense at all to me.
I dream journeys over and over.
Suits me – if I can stay here.
I'm agoraphobic.

THEA: When we were kids they took us every year to the
beach. Big Sur.
Calvin – that's my brother – went for the surf. I went for
the rock. Spent hours tasting salt and touching rock.
Know how long it takes to make a rock?
Me neither.
I hate head stuff. Fourth grade shit.
Rock grades - they make sense to me.
On rock, I compete with myself.
I stood for hours on the beach and asked – with my body
– which way?

She dances a route up the rock.

Rock answers –
If you learn to listen.
One day I leave the ground forever.
I curl my finger tips round a lip and it hooks me like a

fish and pulls me up out of the water – into myself. I'm suspended, gasping. I look down and there's a place to put my foot. Rocked over millennia just to be there, now – for me. Like a friend, you know? Meeting me halfway. I fell in love.

She fumbles with the ice.

It makes him mad.
Me, climbing.

T: Is that why you do it?

THEA: Maybe. If I can get the hang of this ice, maybe I can climb some.
But look – no faults. How's a girl to get a hold?
You here through the season?

T: Most seasons.

THEA: This your job?

T: I have others.

THEA: Don't you hate all this waiting around?

T: Do you?

THEA: Gotten so bored in my life, waiting for other people. This mountaineering shit – nothing to it. Hiking on ice. Sport for dead people.

T: Why are you here?

THEA shrugs.

THEA: Work.

GEORGES, wearing shorts, T-shirt and a red beret, arrives at Base Camp with his gear.

And fun.
Lom-bear! You made it!

GEORGES: *Veni, amore!*

She runs into his arms.

THEA: You look older than I remember,

He takes his cap off.

And thinner.

GEORGES: Disappointed?

THEA: Sure am. You're a whole lot better in my fantasies. Wait till you hear them.

She kisses him passionately.

Do you have any water?

GEORGES presents her with a drinking bottle. She drinks lustily.

Presents?

GEORGES presents her with a book.

Poetry. Great! I'll leave it on the top.
You're beautiful.
This is the boss: Da Tenzing.
This is…?

T: T.

GEORGES: ?

T: T. Robin Truman.

GEORGES: Georges Lambert.

T shakes his hand.

T: Lambert?

GEORGES: Yes. You've heard it before?

T smiles and leaves them.

THEA: You're late. We've been up and down the Fall three times. I'm acclimatised. Native. I'll beat you up there, Georges.

GEORGES kisses her.

GEORGES: Feel my pulse.
See?
Strong as a boy of twenty three.

THEA: Too bad. I like my men older.

GEORGES: You're beautiful.

They embrace.

DA TENZING: Tomorrow we go to Camp One and maybe stay. Move up the glacier.

GEORGES: I'm ready.

GEORGES and THEA take his gear to the tent.

SOPHIE is trying to ring GEORGES. She turns the phone off.

SOPHIE: In my dream:
I see black shaggy beasts like small, sullen mammoths, being driven from a prehistoric pasture.
I hear hooves scraping the stones. Harnesses jangling. Men shouting and cursing and laughing. Black men and white men. Haggling.
I see loads being flung over backs and wind whipping coloured flags over yellow tents. There are jet birds picking at the rubbish or ripping overhead – squealing and somersaulting.
I see towers of turquoise ice sliced by black ravines with silver threads stitching across the gaps.
Cross my heart – and hope to die.
Then I glide on up a silent valley with scraped walls. Hot white light bounces everywhere until my skin is burning. Then I reach an ice face. Cold. Closed.

That's as far as I've seen because at that moment I look down and through the ice a man appears. Naked. White as angels.
Fades up towards me through the ice.
I lie down beside him, but I can't get him warm. He always ignores me. When I touch his mouth it comes apart in pieces like a puzzle. He seems lost in his own pain.
I say 'It's just the same for me, you know'.
He says nothing.

T approaches in his white coat

And who knows if it is anyway? – the same for me I mean.
Looking up I see the strangest thing of all – and not quite clear.
It's alive.
Moving.
Red muscles firing under white skin.
A great, white dream in the sky.

T: (*To SOPHIE.*) Please come through, Mrs Lambert.
Sorry to keep you waiting.
Is no-one with you?

SOPHIE: (*Afraid.*) Do I need someone?

T: …a relative or friend?

SOPHIE: Just me. Should there be someone else?

T: That's my question.

SOPHIE: Do I trust you?

T: Should you trust me?

SOPHIE: Do I know you?

T: Relax. Put this on.

He hands her a white hospital gown and arranges to take an x-ray.

SOPHIE: (*Removing her clothes and putting the gown on.*)
I haven't been in hospital since I had my daughter. The
only good thing about it was the bath. They let me have
a bath. That's the last good thing about it I remember.
The midwife had a grudge. Couldn't tell if it was just
against me, or childbearing women in general. Whatever,
I went to pieces almost at once. All my NCT breathing
skills – out the window. I could only remember how the
NCT teacher found out my husband took photographs
and said she'd once done wet T-shirt shots.
My first husband.
My second husband might have sorted her out. He has
that kind of eyebrow – you know? Presence.
Just now he has Absence.

*DA TENZING is still moving gear. GEORGES is testing
his own oxygen levels with a machine.*

GEORGES: Eighty eight per cent. See?
I can do this without a mask.

THEA: I say if you've got the gear, flaunt it.

GEORGES: It matters to me – absolutely: quality of process.
Two fingers to the bastard timeclock in the genes.

THEA: Miss me?

GEORGES: My dear…my dear…

*GEORGES kisses THEA and they retire to his tent. DA
TENZING comes to his tent and casts a dour glance in their
direction, settling down to boil water.*

Night begins to fall.

SOPHIE fumbles in her bag and dials on her phone again.

*Phone rings in GEORGES' tent. THEA unravels herself
from GEORGES and extracts the phone.*

GEORGES: Hey!

THEA: I gave my editor your mobile. You don't mind.
Hello? Doug?
No one there.

*GEORGES takes it from her and turns it off. A terrible
howl fills the air and everyone freezes but GEORGES.*

What the hell?

GEORGES: Those things are as lethal as an AK-47. One
went off in the theatre once – in the pants of a press man.
The surgeon's hand jumped. He nearly sliced through
the aorta.

THEA: What the fuck was that noise?

GEORGES: What noise? Yak?

THEA: Oh, sure. Yak.

GEORGES: Crow? Snow leopard?

THEA: Snow leopards have publicity phobias. They don't
yell. Didn't you research?

*THEA leaves the tent to look. In the shadows round the bed,
T is confronting the YETI, SOPHIE, who is tearing out
wires and hurling objects, howling.*

SOPHIE: I knew she wouldn't leave us alone. I knew. I knew.

T: Sophie, Sophie –

He presents a paper bag.

Breathe.

She breathes into the bag.

SOPHIE: Where have you been?
Looking inside me.
And?

T: Another time.

SOPHIE: I'm hurting. Hurting. Where is he?

T: I'm here.

SOPHIE: And who the merry fuck are you?

T: Sophie…

SOPHIE: I'm so afraid.

GEORGES is pouring drinks.

THEA approaches DA TENZING.

THEA: You heard it? What was it? A Yeti?

DA TENZING: Sometimes the mountain –

THEA: What?

No response.

Bad omen?

He nods.

Wait.

She takes the bottle off GEORGES and takes it to DA TENZING.

From a bad wo-man.
Make a friendship cup with the men.

DA TENZING hesitates.

It's Grappa.

GEORGES: The best. Oaked.

THEA: He can buy more down the drug store. Go on.

DA TENZING takes it. THEA returns to the tent.

GEORGES: Any more of my supplies you'd like to give
away?

THEA: What you got?

She rifles through his rucksack.

GEORGES: Marmot.

THEA: What?

GEORGES: They get inside tents and turn everything over. Little. Like prairie dogs – rounder.

THEA: We have bears, Lom-bear, in America. Big. Like bears – meaner.

More rifling.

Lime. You fear scurvy? No: Gin! Heavenly man. Tonic?

GEORGES: Impractical. Too heavy. Use the snow.

THEA: Base Camp snow?

GEORGES: Thinning and reduction of temperature combined.

THEA: Coffee! A coffee percolator!
Sainte Georges! Not good for the head though. You'll get into trouble with da Goering.

THEA finds a photo in his rucksack.

Your wife?

Hiatus. GEORGES takes the photo. She burrows on.

Truffles.

She starts eating them.

Great pick-a-nick basket, Lom-bear.

She toasts him.

To our journey.

GEORGES: To the conquest of Everest.

THEA: Hey – it's been done a time or two, didn't they tell you?

GEORGES: Not by me. And that's what counts.

THEA: You know: you can always judge by first impressions.

GEORGES: And what were your first impressions?

THEA: Email don't count. You need to hear the voice. Smell the sweat. See the cut of his shirt and the flow of his money. What momma taught me.

GEORGES: And?

THEA: You're fun to be with. Make me laugh: it's all I ask.

GEORGES: Good girl.

THEA: No expectations.

GEORGES: No?

THEA: Want me to have some?

GEORGES touches her hair.

GEORGES: I don't know.
I love my wife.

THEA: (*Looking at the photograph.*) She's younger than I thought. Pretty.

GEORGES: That isn't her.

DA TENZING goes to the cairn.

DA TENZING: Sherpas get to the top all the time. Sherpas die all the time. Ghosts when they die. Ghosts when they live. Born to climb mountains, we don't see why they need to be climbed. Only for money. We carry the round eyes (*Shrugs toward GEORGES' tent.*) up to the top on

our shoulders. We call them just another load. Why not give us their clothes and we can wear their clothes to the top? Same thing. It's not we are the ghosts, maybe. They see plenty up there – ghosts – the white ones. Right after they see their first dead body. It blows them away. We see the bodies every year as we set the ropes. They become friends.
Like stones that mark the way.
Tell us we aren't lost.

Explosion like untamped gunpowder. Sound of an avalanche like gunfire. Soft screams of ghost men as on a ghost battlefield.

Nine sherpa. Nine men. All from our village. The monsoon comes early. Bad forecast. Mallory goes anyway. Avalanche. All the English survive. Two Sherpa swim. Seven drown and go to sleep in the great snow tent that sets like stone. Underneath our feet: sleeping men, rocked in snow – each one alone. Together.

T: (*Still to SOPHIE.*) That makes you angry.

DA TENZING: (*Shrugs.*) It's happened forever. Nothing can make it good. Or bad.
She wouldn't let Mallory go home again. After that. They're children of the mountain now, and so is he.

DA TENZING goes back to preparing a meal.

T: (*To SOPHIE.*) Take a deep breath and hold.
We need to get to the bottom of what's going on inside you.

He goes to his camera on the tripod.

THEA positions herself in front of the summit backdrop.

DA TENZING is squeezing flour cakes.

SOPHIE takes a deep breath.

THEA: I'm Me-a. Reporter for the Westerly Eagle Sun.

Sure – my passport says Thea. Dorothea. Gift of God.
Ha.
Mom had her one and only milk punch in Amherst.
Scotch with milk and sugar. Packs a wallop. Lost her
virginity to Dad there and then and: here comes Me-a:
Theodora. Gift of God on the Rocks.
Madonna with a headache.

SOPHIE lets her breath out.

Then she split. My Mom.

T photographs THEA. She goes to write on her laptop.

T: (*To SOPHIE.*) Again.

GEORGES positions himself in front of the backdrop.

SOPHIE takes a breath and holds it.

GEORGES: Georges Lambert. Medical technician.
Some men write their names on maps. Mine's written on
the heart: *Le Pont Lambert.*
Americans call it the Lambert Valve. Do I care?
I'm Swiss – which god knows is a linguistic challenge in
itself.
I speak French, German, English and Italian. Fluently.
And, of course, American.

*He pulls out flags: French, German, English, Italian, American
and finally Swiss flag.*

Work's my passion.

SOPHIE lets out her breath.

T photographs GEORGES who then goes back to his tent.

T: Last time.

SOPHIE positions herself in front of the backdrop.

SOPHIE: Sophie Lambert: patient and agoraphobic.

And I'm afraid of heights. Especially flying.
If God had intended us to fly – we'd've been born with
airmiles.
Georges climbs. Risks his life. Why?
Don't know why.
Know how:
I stay here.
At the crossroads.

T photographs SOPHIE then sets the timer on his camera.

T: T. Robin Truman. Ice Fall Doctor. Amateur photographer.
A little old for such shenanigans now, but with a wealth
of experience behind me and an attachment to mountain
landscapes.
And a camera.
The camera: once so rare, now an object of democracy.
You'll all have one, and when you journey, photograph
the journey.

He takes his own photograph.

As photographers, we are all agents of death.
Also agents of resurrection.
Our pictures travel through space and time, floating the
dead or distant object up to the future, sinking the
subject (us) back into the past.

He photographs the audience.

Trust me.
I'm a photographer.

The Ice Fall

Stupa stage 2: water.

*THEA is at her laptop, which is connected by multifarious wires to
a huge battery etc.*

*T is doctoring the Ice Fall ladder connections. After a while,
GEORGES goes to help.*

THEA: (*Typing copy.*) 'Water's all you think about up here.
You wake up – you're thirsty. You get dressed – you're
thirsty. Pick your nose – you're thirsty. How the hell
you claw up over eight thousand metres without a water
hydrant plumbed to Katmandu in your pack, God
knows.
You have breakfast and the food glues your throat shut
unless you wash it down with gallons of disgusting tea.
Yes. Tea. How low can a girl from Boston sink? You take
a walk – you're thirsty. You admire the scenery – you're
thirsty. In between drinks you think about eating humble
snow – milk of the mountain goddess – and your *Sirdar*
says "People piss as near the tents as possible."
Paragraph.
A *Sirdar* is the chief Sherpa. Ours is called Da
Tenzing. Remember the famous Tenzing? That photo
on the summit like the man on the moon? Knew how
to get his body ready for a photograph, Tenzing
Norgay. Bet he was dynamite in bed. Our Tenzing's
altogether a different cookie: hard to bite. Trust me,
I've tried.

Pause.

'We all cough like consumptives in an Alpine sanatorium.
We all have the shits.
At least that means I can eat and eat (which I do) and
still lose pounds.
Come to Base Camp Health Farm and get that boyish
body.

Pause.

'I hear my readers asking:
Where's the John at Base Camp? Base Camp is the

John. Like being on a boat. Nowhere to go and everyone to see you going. Except on a boat you shit into the sea. Here the sea is solid ice. "Water, water everywhere and not a drop to drink…" I am lost on the mean glass ocean with icebergs bigger than the Titanic ever tipped her hat to. Blue-green serac towers, leaning down on you like Manhattan skyscrapers after too much booze. Waiting centuries for that once in a lifetime moment – to fall on you.

The Bronx kids are mountain ravens, goraks, scavenging on the shit of climbers who have paid thousands of dollars and trained years to spend ten weeks in a very rough neighborhood indeed.

Rich pickings.

Pause.

'I hear my readers calling from the other side of the world: "cut the crap, Thea, and spill the beans: Is there really fucking at Base Camp?"
Well, let me tell you – Base Camp is permanently fucked.

Pause.

'Sometimes though I come out my tent early in the morning – everyone's asleep – the sun is out of sight and turning the snow peaks rose-gold. It feels like I'm alone to see the first dawn of the world…'

Pause. She pushes button.

Send.

She tries to send the text.

GEORGES: (*To T.*) She makes me smile.
The things she says.
Never heard a woman say such things.

No response from T.

Love this sort of thing.
Reminds me of work.
Did you have Meccano when you were a boy?

THEA: My head hurts.

No response from DA TENZING.

I'm dying of thirst.

DA TENZING: I'm making tea.

THEA: (*British.*) Tea and crampons, Carruthers.

DA TENZING: Tibetan tea.

THEA: Did the men enjoy the grappa?

DA TENZING: Americans fly in and get headaches. Sherpa walk for days, drink all night – no headache.

THEA: 'Yes thanks, Thea – we partied all night – it was great.'

Pause as she struggles with the machinery.

Sure we fly in. We have lives elsewhere.

DA TENZING: You have headaches.
You should sleep more – if you want to get to the top.

THEA: You sound like Dad when my grades are going down and he catches me sneaking in at five a.m.

Pause.

'Want to reach the summit girls and boys – keep your legs crossed. No sex please – we're Sherpa.'
Not what I heard. Alice Dodge comes back here every year for a workout and never gets higher than Base Camp.
Maine's Merry Widow, Alice.
Sends her love.

She tries to send copy.

Joke.
But you never know…

DA TENZING: Stealing lives.

THEA: Me? Just writing off taxes.
How can I write an investigation if I don't investigate?
This isn't working.
I need to wire my editor.

DA TENZING: The batteries are re-charging.

THEA: Again! Shit. My text has gone. Where?
Shit.
Shit.
Why are the batteries drained?

DA TENZING: (*Reluctant.*) Downloaded an eight-page
email this morning.

THEA: Eight? Eight-page emails to Everest Base Camp?
Who's it for?

She looks at the pages.

Oh –

GEORGES: I was born in the mountains.
Where I come from, mountains bring people together.
We're neutral. The Swiss flag unites Europe in the cross.

DA TENZING: I didn't think he'd want to be disturbed, so
I printed it.

THEA: Thanks, Mom.
Fix this up will you? I'm behind as it is and my editor's
a shithead.

DA TENZING obliges.

GEORGES: It's my trade – building bridges. Electronic
engineering in Geneva to Biophysics in California – to
this. A glorious logic, building things.

THEA: My last draft's gone.
  All that breathless prose – dispersed among the stardust.
  Maybe God's proofing it.

  DA TENZING reacts.

  Excuse me.
  Which is worse on the mountain? Sex or blasphemy?

DA TENZING: You'll be on line soon.

  He starts to cook. Smells of garlic and cumin fill the air.

  THEA glances at the email pages. She is profoundly restless.

GEORGES: Are you married?

  T doesn't reply.

  I married too young. The hippy days. Crazy. It fell
  apart. I wasn't ready. She remarried fast, twice: some
  builder from Connecticut who beat up on her and then
  an asshole Englishman. Had two more children. I still
  ring her.
  Every New Year.
  I waited for the right sort of love to come along, and
  focused on work.
  You've heard of the Lambert Valve?

THEA: Why are you doing the cooking? You're the boss.

DA TENZING: I like to cook.

THEA: Play cards?
  We could play for cookies. Or we could play for real.
  Strip poker. What do you say?
  Biscuits, Carruthers? Or death?

  No response.

  OK. We keep our clothes on this time.

  No response.

WhadIdo now?
Ohhh, I said 'death'.
It was a joke.
Does everything spook you?

Pause.

DA TENZING cups his hands.

DA TENZING: I have drunk tea from a *Ya-te* skull.

Pause.

THEA: Darjeeling or Earl Grey?

GEORGES: Work's my passion, not mountaineering. Climbing a mountain's like climbing a woman: good exercise.

GEORGES lies down to sunbathe.

THEA: My throat hurts.

DA TENZING brings her some tea. She dips her finger in the scum on top.

DA TENZING: Yak butter.

THEA: Sure.

She hands it back.

You forgot the skull.

Communications crackle.

GHOST OF THEA'S EDITOR is heard.

GHOST OF THEA'S EDITOR: Thea, this is school assignment crap. You haven't even read this take – it's full of typos. I need clean copy. Take it back and fix it, or if hypoxia's set in already, send it to John to proof. While you're there, my newshole for this is 35 inches and this is 40, darling. Lose five inches, add more quotes, underline the break-outs and give me a two-line head.

THEA: A two-line head.
   OK asshole:
   'Eagle Sun reporter sits on butt
   While mountain strolls away.'

Restless, she picks up GEORGES' email papers.

DA TENZING goes back to cooking.

SOPHIE: I think he asked me – do I have anything to
   come back for? It may have been to go back for – I'm
   not sure now I think of it. I was going to reply: what
   exactly are you driving at? when the word 'driving'
   lodged in my head so I didn't say anything at all.
   I'm wheeling down the valley of another dream.
   A dream of driving.

THEA: I emailed Georges when we knew we were both on
   this trip. We had an e-ffair. We both have a Way with
   Words. Met up first time in the Alps at his favourite
   place: Valle Paradiso. (*She chuckles*.) Told me he'd told his
   wife he was meeting his sister in Switzerland. In fact, he
   did meet his sister first – at least, he told me it was his
   sister. How do I know?

SOPHIE: I dream I'm driving north towards the Alps.
   Towards Valle Paradiso, and missing the turn on one of
   those terrifying major Italian arterial routes that power
   towards France through the bowels of the mountains.

THEA: What's a sister anyway?

GEORGES: When I met Sophie I met my rock. My anchor.
   I'm so strong, with Sophie. It gives me great flexibility.
   I can bend and bend and never break. (*Listens*.) She's
   flexible too. Great imagination. (*Shouts*.) Hello!

ECHO: Hellohellohellohellohellohellohello…

THEA: Maybe he met two lovers in one week.

She shrugs and grins.

I guess two heads are better than one.

THEA brings GEORGES his email.

GEORGES: There's an amazing echo if you stand just here. Try it.

THEA: (*Shouts.*) Calvin!

ECHO: Calvincalvincalvincalvincalvincalvin…

GEORGES: (*Not reading email.*) So much paper. I was clearing out stuff before I left – old letters, photos. One woman wrote she'd left her husband and was waiting for me. Somewhere.

He smiles.

Unsigned. Know what?

THEA: You don't recall her name.

GEORGES: Isn't that terrible?

THEA: Yep. Might still be there. Waiting.

THEA goes back to her lap top.

GEORGES: Who's Calvin?

SOPHIE: I know by now we've missed the turn to Valle Paradiso – but I daren't tell him. He's driving. I see him out of the corner of my eye: he's younger than me. A bit. But that's a lot, a bit, at our age. I think – yes – he's my lover.

She's delighted.

I'm having an affair.
My first affair.
We have to drive on and I try to read the map. It's hard without my reading glasses and it dawns on me rather

too slowly with a sinking in my stomach there are no
more turnings this side of the Mont Blanc Tunnel. We
can't turn off until we've done the tunnel, crossed an
invisible line in the heart of the rock, and reached
another country.

DA TENZING: It's time to eat.

*T and DA TENZING start laying a table. T lights a candle.
(Cf. "Table laid for a meal": heliograph on glass by Niepce,
1829.)*

SOPHIE: It all seemed very continental somehow. In
England if you miss a turn it's the difference between
Reading and Newbury.

T: This illumination of a candle – what's the verb? Flatters?
Suggests? Seduces? Promises? – which is both a verb
and a noun, plural.

SOPHIE, GEORGES and THEA advance to the table.

See how the shadows around the light have deepened?
Candlelight – masks?
Can't…
Leave it.
Man and woman sit across the table from each other –
the lucky ones – and between them – the lucky ones – is
decent food, bottled water, soft music, finger bowls, a
flower hopefully of the real and therefore scented
variety, good wine (red as a rule of thumb, unless it's
fish, and even then, Americans can surprise us), and: a
candle to hold to it.
One thing I know for a fact candlelight does do is
conceal the nature of the skin. Smoothes like powder
snow over laughter lines at the eye corners, over the
brow crevasse of a frown. Also – hair. Now this is a little
more ambiguous. At this time of life, heaven decrees a
strange decree: that men will in general grow less hairy

and women, more so – as though the genders are destined to arc towards each other on a hirsute parabola. To touch and fuse? To pass like ships in the night? You observe though through candlelight, gentled gaze, that the balding man frames somehow less bald and a woman's facial growth is spirited away.
Like a cunning photographer after the event, candlelight retouches.

THEA sits opposite GEORGES. T sits opposite SOPHIE. DA TENZING serves the meal.

The Restaurant Dance

GEORGES/T: (*To THEA/SOPHIE.*) You wear a ring. Do you have a husband? A lover?

THEA/SOPHIE: (*To GEORGES/T.*) You wear a ring too.

THEA: (*To GEORGES.*) A team of us spent three months digging into the politics of the tunnel under Boston Harbor. It was awesome down there. Lost sight of what it was all about though. Fell in with the guy who ran the drill.

She points at a wine on the wine list to DA TENZING.

DA TENZING: That's red.

THEA: So?

DA TENZING: You ordered fish.

THEA: So?

DA TENZING shrugs and fetches red wine.

SOPHIE: (*To T.*) My husband doesn't understand me.

THEA: (*To GEORGES.*) Shoulders out here and eyes like a fawn under the cedars.
I have rocks from the Big Dig on my desk at home.
He has my pen. Maybe.

GEORGES: (*To THEA.*) What was his name…?

THEA shrugs.

T: (*To SOPHIE.*) Funny you should say that.

SOPHIE: (*To T.*) Why?

THEA: (*To GEORGES.*) Plenty of rocks, eh, Georges?
Plenty of pens.

GEORGES: (*To THEA.*) …Calvin?

T: (*To SOPHIE.*) My wife doesn't understand me either.
In fact –

THEA: (*To GEORGES.*) Dave. Dave Lawrence.

T: (*To SOPHIE.*) – no-one does.

THEA: (*To GEORGES.*) Jealous?

GEORGES: (*To THEA.*) I'm never jealous.

SOPHIE: (*To T.*) Are we lovers?
This is a dream, you see, but I think…

THEA: (*To GEORGES.*) What about your wife?

SOPHIE: …my co-ordinates are a bit hazy.

GEORGES: (*To THEA.*) Sophie? She can do as she likes.
I wouldn't mind. I want her to be happy – like I am right
now: utterly – happy.

SOPHIE: (*To T.*) Georges?

T rises from the table.

T: Man and woman. Across the table. Husband and wife of
twenty-five years more-or-less exemplary union –
hungry? Lovers on their first night, just prior to mating,
or on their last night, before separating, who can't
swallow anything? Brother and sister, incestuous? Client

and whore? Client and gigolo? Just good friends sat in mutual consolation?

THEA reaches out and touches GEORGES' face lightly.

Beloved: /I love you.

THEA: /I love you.

T: At least – I love, in this manifestation, you.
(For I have been ere now a fish, fowl, rock, cataract, reptile, stone, bone, travel agent and even a woman).
Tonight I am all man, however, and I love you.
/Sleep with me.

GEORGES: /Sleep with me.

T: And we may mean sleep.
At our age.

SOPHIE is trying to read a map like a menu. She takes out her glasses.

SOPHIE: Thanks to me we're stuck on the autobahn, heading for the Mont Blanc Tunnel. I love maps but somehow I've always been shit at reading them – glasses or no glasses. He's younger than me. A bit. But that's a lot, a bit, at our age, when the older's a woman. I mean, girls are born ancient anyway – age by osmosis from gazing into the sad eyes of our mothers.
I don't want to spend the first few hours with him in reading glasses.
He might start worrying I take my teeth out at bedtime.

DA TENZING: We climb!

THEA straps on her crampons under supervision from DA TENZING. GEORGES goes back to his tent to gather his and THEA's gear.

THEA: Dance?

DA TENZING doesn't respond. She stomps around.

Claws. I'm a yeti. Have you seen one? You're seeing one now.
Was that a yeti howled last night?
Hello?
Anyone there?
Why won't you talk with me?

DA TENZING: Talk? I talk.

THEA: No talk. How old are you anyway? 108?

He ignores her, checking her gear.

You hate us don't you?
Is it all punters or just Westerners? Or just Americans? Or just women? Or just women with mouths?

DA TENZING: We respect all souls as though they are our own.

THEA: And just how do you pull that off?

DA TENZING: We are taught: treat everyone as though they are your mother.

THEA mimes loading her ice pick.

THEA: Lock 'n' Load…

DA TENZING: ?

THEA: My friend – back home that would be a mandate for mass murder.

She gets on the ladder, aims her ice pick and does automatic gunfire.

Rdudududududud. Die. Die. Die.

Her noise is overtaken by the faint sound of an avalanche.

Silence.

What's that?

DA TENZING: Snow sliding on the Face.

THEA: Hey! – the ladder moved.

DA TENZING: Get off it. GET OFF IT!

He pulls her off.

THEA: Jesus.
How deep down there?

DA TENZING: (*Shrugs.*) We say – all the way to America.

THEA: Hi, Dad! How's business?
Will I turn round in the middle or shoot out feet first?
I guess it's academic. I guess in the middle, I fry.

SOPHIE: The strangest, quite the strangest thing, after a
while, is: I notice there are no other cars. No lorries. No
traffic. No more olive-skinned Italian prostitutes in
lay-bys dressed in a lime green sort of uniform that kicks
out onto the freeway truckers' watering eyes. I watched
him – my lover – out of the corner of my eye – as we
passed them, for his reaction. I know he's had a lot of
women. He told me straight away. He said nothing until
we passed the fifth whore and then he sucks some air up
between his teeth, tosses his forelock and says 'maybe we
could hire one to drive the car for us while we get in the
back.'

THEA pulls a glove off and starts to write in her notebook.

DA TENZING: Keep your gloves on.

THEA: Know my favourite mountain story? Alice goes up
to this guy, a monk, sitting bare-ass-naked on a rock near
Mount Meru, meditating.
She takes his photograph. He smiles. She smiles. They
talk a little. She's just charmed to death.
'Gee' she says in the end, 'I wish I could take you back

with me to see New York.'

'Lady,' he says, 'I am New York.'

SOPHIE: Like the toss of a unicorn's head in a Sunday
park it takes my breath away. So not English.
Except, of course – I've never had an English lover.
Only an English husband. Maybe they burst out of their
cocoons in the same way like powder moths and dance
with the flames of passion and get singed too, away from
their sad wives.
So.
What is this game we're playing?
Do I want to wake up?
Is there anything to go back for? he said.

T comes up to THEA.

T: You're a writer.

THEA: I'm an investigative journalist. So watch your step.

T: I'm an investigative photographer. Can I be of assistance?

THEA: Sure.

T: Prints? Transparencies? Colour? Black and white?

THEA: Bit of a saturated market though. I mean everyone
climbs it and everyone writes about it. If I'd wanted to
do original research it would've made more sense to stay
home and experience the shopping centre in Mystic.
Actually, this is a bit like the shopping centre in Mystic.
Just – more death and litter.

T: Time magazine? National Geographic?

THEA: Westerly Eagle Sun.

T: Black and white then.

THEA: Excuse me. Perfect colour only. I can get you 50
bucks a negative. Your copyright. If they print it.

T: If? They'd send you all the way up here and not print it?

THEA: They pay me peanuts – but it's two thousand dollars when a major takes it over.

T: Your trip cost sixty four thousand dollars.

THEA: And the answer to the question is: Dad. Dad's the answer. And Georges. Dad wants a picture of me on the summit of the world for his desk at Junk Wool Corporate Headquarters. Georges wants to relive his youth.

T: What do you want?

THEA: Cheesy stuff. No Nepalese dreamstuff. Pissed-in snow. Shit and empty cans. Plastic.
A line I guess.

T: Of…?

THEA: Punters. Like in '96. Lining up on the Hillary step in a British kind of way: queueing for a British kind of death.

T: Americans don't queue?

THEA: Never heard the word. Stationary persecution.

DA TENZING: We move across now.

THEA: Me first!

She gets on the ladder.

(*To T.*) A body in the foreground would be cool…

GEORGES comes out of the tent in full gear.

GEORGES: Waited years for this moment.
Had this sort of feeling – before – like when sliding doors open at an airport and she's there – someone you want to see, then, more than you want to breathe.
Prepare for months to see, but still, not ready – in the moment.

My mouth's dry. I feel like a boy.
Will she really be there?

SOPHIE: He says: come with me. Leave them and fly, he says. Dance with me.

She gets up.

I so want to dance.
So I say: Yes.
I'll leave them behind me.

She dances in a formal way with an invisible partner.

THEA: (*To T.*) ...that cheesy.

SOPHIE: I don't mention my fear of flying. Think he'll cure me: take me everywhere. With him. But some things never change.

DA TENZING: We climb.

He goes to the next ladder to check it.

THEA: (*To T.*) He comes out every morning to work on this. Every morning the stuff's moved. The flags are wrong. The ladders tip. How can something this huge and solid fucking move?

T: It's a river.

THEA: Where's the fish?

T: Us. Climbing back to source. She's a wave – Everest; it's only that we move too fast to see her flowing. We just need to switch to a different timetrack, that's all. Slow down.

THEA: You serious? My butt has barnacles. Up and down and rest. Up and down and rest. I want up and up and up.

She balances on the ladder.

T: Human kind cannot bear too much verticality.

THEA: Watch me!

She does a handstand on the ladder.

GEORGES: What are you doing?

THEA: Hi Dad. Hi America.

He pulls her off. She's laughing.

GEORGES: Fool.

THEA: Hey –

GEORGES: Why do you take so many stupid risks?

THEA: You don't?

GEORGES: I'm in control of the risks. You're –

THEA: I'm – ?

He hasn't let go of her.

GEORGES: Reckless…

THEA: Let go Georges. It's not your business what I do.

He lets go of her.

(*To T.*) Photograph this. Cover of 'Time'.

She goes on over the ladder.

T: What is your business, anyway?

GEORGES: Mending hearts.

He laughs drily.

Le Pont Lambert,
Looks – like a snowflake.
Like a piece of Meccano.
Connects the major artery.

GEORGES follows THEA: first on foot, then he crawls across.

T: A terrible thing at our age.

DA TENZING: ?

T: Falling.
(*Stepping onto the ladder.*) 'The path of Love is as a strand of hair over an abyss of fire'.
I say things like that.
No one listens.

THEA and GEORGES climb slowly over the Ice Fall to a vantage point where Everest is visible. GHOST OF MALLORY appears.

GHOST OF MALLORY: Presently the miracle happens.
A preposterous triangular lump rises out of the depths; its edge leaping at an angle of seventy degrees and ending nowhere. To the left a black serrated crest hangs in the sky. Incredibly. Gradually, very gradually, we see the great mountain sides and glaciers and arêtes, now one fragment and now another through the floating rifts, until far higher in the sky than imagination has dared suggest, the white summit of Everest appears.
And in this series of partial glimpses we see a whole; we're able to piece together the fragments as they coalesce.
Piece together the dream.

GEORGES: Always waiting for me. Here in this moment: a miracle.

THEA: Shit.
How can we climb that?

GEORGES: Aching to climb her. She's aching to be climbed.

DA TENZING and T are still at the ladder.

DA TENZING: I don't remember her face. No picture in here.

Only her head bent over the mud people. Her hair is black but with rainbows like gorak feathers. Her arms when she runs wave like wings. Like she will fly. I run to fly with her. I don't catch her up.

T: Where would you fly?

DA TENZING: Over the mountain. Higher than the peak. We would circle together, looking at the people. Looking for Lord Siva. Looking for chocolate and biscuits and lollies.
Some day.
Maybe.

T: There's a tent. There's a mountain. Up above: satellites pull triangles of lines between one voice and another. In the web, we fly, my friend. Always. Give me your hand.

T helps DA TENZING across the ladder.

DA TENZING: No more coming back. Tonight we stay at Camp One.

T: And take tea, little brother?

DA TENZING smiles for the first time.

DA TENZING: Hot chocolate, *tondai.*

They cross out of the space.

SOPHIE moves across and stands in the chasm.

Machinery crackles and Jehovah speaks.

GHOST OF THEA'S EDITOR: Thea? You there? What's your lead? Where's your opening? What the hell's the story? Communicate, sweetheart. Composing's getting restless. Do you want me to close this issue without your first piece? Get real, Thea.

(*Aside.*) Shit. We'll have to fill in.

Thea? Thea? You listening…?

Interval is Camp One.

Audience follow the actors out over the ladders.

The climbing actors stay in character in the space intermingling with the audience, taking hot chocolate and Tibetan sweets. The audience is invited to be photographed in front of the summit of the mountain – all shots of people at the summit are vital for the denouement, so someone spends the interval getting them ready for the slideshow at the end.

End of Act One.

ACT TWO

Scenes from higher up the Mountain

MALLORY's cairn is still there. There's now a down – clothed body in the space. PUNDITS are operating on SOPHIE, or the mountain. T is using his tripod as a theodolite. Body sounds: heartbeat, breathing, medical bleeps etc.

T: Ever wonder about the word 'pundit'? Probably not. Not to worry. It's no more or less important than any other word.
It's from the Hindi of course.
Like pyjamas.
And bungalow.
It means any learned man now: any expert.
When men of authority and learning decide to measure the world by triangulation and define its boundaries and which segment's whose, the British Army employ pundits as spies to penetrate the great and secret spaces of The Himalaya. *Hima* – of the snow. *Alaya* – home.

Lantern slide: PUNDITS triangulating.

In 1823 the Superintendent of the Indian Trigonometrical Survey is one Colonel Sir George Everest.

Slide: Colonel Sir George Everest.

In these days there are mountains beyond sight to be measured – still belonging to the primordial world of the imagination, for to walk ten miles over Shambhala takes not only weeks, or months, but crosses aeons of geology and culture. Off the map.
(*Smiles.*) 'There be dragons'.

Slide: drawing by Vigne 1834 of triangulation in India.
These pundits – these wise men – these secret agents, alchemists and men of knowledge, Indian, but with the

somatic features of the mountain people, take up their sextants, theodolites, pencils and notebooks and hide them in their walking sticks; learn to assess altitudes according to the boiling of water and their bearings by the stars; measure distance by counting their paces and rig the Buddhist rosary to have one hundred beads instead of the customary one-oh-eight. If they are discovered – and in Shambhala all strangers are known at once – this discrepancy of eight is a matter of life and death. Some never return to report their findings, theories or even starving visions to Colonel Sir George Everest; or to his successor.

For lo, even as I speak, Colonel Sir George Everest ups and dies, and is succeeded.

Then one day, like a distant planet unseen on the edge of the galaxy, a theoretical place burns its shadows onto the snow-dazzled mind of one pundit, Sikhdar, and the image which develops in the fluid of his speculation seems quite surprisingly, unexpectedly high. Very high in theory – very high indeed. At least one hundred feet higher than the last contender. Probably, arguably, theoretically, the highest place on earth. For Sikhdar – the sacred peak where Siva and Kali will be found embracing. For the British: the Third Pole.

Could the goal to end all goals but two have finally been pinpointed? Would we soon know and thereby somehow own, another top of the world? We fuck up over the South Pole in a very British way, and the North Pole doesn't bear thinking about. Will this be third time lucky?

The British, ever a cautious race, duly note her in their triangulation with a question mark and call this theoretical triangle of rock, which lies beyond all horizons and draws its sister mountains round it like a cloak:

Peak XV.

Slide: *of Everest.*

SOPHIE: I've always been afraid of heights…

T: The pundits go on stalking her like a wild beast, like the snow leopard that is seldom if ever to be seen, like a nesting bird guarding impossibly valuable eggs if only one could fright her from her nest long enough to blow them for market. Proof of her existence is worth a lot of money to the pundits. What on earth is it worth to the English? you may cry. Why – speak not of profit – 'twould be the jewel in the crown of the Raj: the queen at the centre of the chess board, the triumphant playing piece in their Great Game with Russia – their Shadow Tournament with China, the coldest of cold wars, fought by ghosts and invisible lines crosshatching across the coldest of cold lands in the world: where India shoulders up the rucking land out of the ocean, climbing the steps of impossible mountains to the wind blistered plateau of Tibet.
A world of ice: frozen, yet moving. Dead, yet a place of primordial life. Cold as a corpse, hot as a desert. Beautiful and painful as love itself.

SOPHIE: …then I dream I'm lying inside a mountain…

T sets up to take photographs on the tripod.

T: Helpless we climb, or lie, in the crucible of merciless alchemical process.

PUNDITS: /Mrs Lambert?
Next of kin?
Health insurance?
Allergy to penicillin?
Any jewellery about your person? etc.

T: (*As PUNDITS speak.*) /I try not to get involved.
It's a job you do for love, not money.

PUNDITS: This will hurt a little.
Count backwards from five, Mrs Lambert.

SOPHIE: /Five, four, three…

T: (*As SOPHIE counts.*) /The higher we go, the more the hours are corrugated into minutes. Time… (*He makes a wave gesture.*) Mountains flow. Life is concertinaed into waves. A day might be a breath or a lifetime. Rule-bending time. Story time.

SOPHIE sits up. PUNDITS disperse to become climbers.

SOPHIE: Beginning middle and end time?

T: Something to cling to when the pain gets bad. Otherwise…

SOPHIE: Do you? Cling?

T: Can't always afford to keep to the path when I have an assignment. But I keep my eye on the ropes. Yes.

SOPHIE: I clung…

T: It's a job you do for love, not safety.

SOPHIE: …clang.

T: Well; love, and to be almost entirely truthful, a desire to observe others whilst remaining aloof. Out of the picture.

SOPHIE: The pain's sliding off my sides. My mind's floating – up.

Valley of Silence

Stupa stage 3: fire.

It is hot. Fierce shadows. ('The valley is a freezer by night, cauldron by day' - ed.)

DA TENZING moves in a series of quick, light steps, breathes, then quick light steps again – almost bouncing. THEA plods like an over-loaded yak. GEORGES paces himself. T photographs them. SOPHIE watches.

GEORGES: (*Continuous with THEA's musings. / Steps. Rests.*)
Two. Three. Four. Breathe. (*Steps. Rests.*) Two. Three. Four.
Breathe.
Lambert. Georges. George. Breathe. Lambert. Georges.
Lambert. Breathe. George. Lambert. Lambert… (*Etc.*)

THEA: (*In mask/simultaneous with GEORGES/ voice over?*) /
There was a lot of mortar missing at my junior high
school. One recess I started climbing the wall, following
the deepest cracks. Made it to the third floor before the
stupid fire truck arrived. The volunteer fireman on the
ladder worked for Dad. He just yanked me off the wall
like he was saving me. Like I was some baby chick.
Asshole. I could have made the roof. The kids were
going nuts. Calvin was a sophomore and his buddies
teased him about having a spider for a sister. He walked
up to me and smacked me with his fist. I didn't hit him
back. That time.

GHOST OF CALVIN: Thea! Come down!

ECHO: Downdowndowndowndowndowndown…

THEA tears off her mask.

THEA: (*Shouts.*) Calvin?

ECHO: Calvincalvincalvincalvincalvincalvincalvin…

DA TENZING fixes her mask back on. They walk on.

SOPHIE: It's a mug's game.

T: What?

SOPHIE: That. Taking photographs. When's now?

T: What?

SOPHIE: Now – when is it? How would you know? Too
busy focusing the camera.
Right.

Suddenly, SOPHIE marches up to the climbers. They freeze like statues, but do not see her.

T: Sophie?

SOPHIE: Time for a change.

She walks round the climbers as at an exhibition.

My dream.
Hello Georges.

She laughs. She goes to a tent.

The sides are breathing. Look.
It changes the colours.

She climbs inside and sits cross-legged like a child.

If I swing one side, the other moves to keep it company.

T: What are you doing, Sophie?
Where are you?

SOPHIE: Something's in here with me, in the air: a
friendly space, breathing.
Don't know what.
Know why.
I'm dying.

T: Sophie?

SOPHIE: Shhh.
How are you Sophie?
Fine.
Just dying.
Shhh.
He's telling me a story.

T: Sophie.
Sophie?

SOPHIE: (*In tent playing hide and seek.*) Ready!

Climbers start to move again.

GEORGES: /Two. Three. Four. Breathe. (*Steps. Rests.*) Two. Three. Four. Breathe.

SOPHIE: (*Simultaneous with GEORGES breathing.*) /Mrs Lambert?
Next of kin?
Health insurance?
Allergy to penicillin?
Any jewellery about your person?

She takes off her wedding ring and throws it out of the tent, laughing. T goes to her. She runs out of the tent, laughing.

You don't scare me any more.

T: Did I scare you?

SOPHIE: I want to play too.

T: So I see.

SOPHIE: I want to play.

T: Sophie: it's an operation you know, any way you play it…

SOPHIE: Doctors and nurses.
I've read the books.
Over 7,000 feet women stop bleeding…

T: …that much I know…

SOPHIE: …so if I'd always lived on a mountain, I'd be a girl. Nothing to lose. I wouldn't be sick at all.

T: …they have to see what's going on inside.

SOPHIE: I've brought a map. Look.

She produces the map from Act One.

Are you angry with me?

T: Angry? It's just…

SOPHIE: Kiss me then.

T kisses her.

T: It's just – you have to have a steady hand in my line of work – and you startled me.

GEORGES: (*Steps. Rests.*) Two. Three. Four. Breathe. (*Steps. Rests.*) Two. Three. Four. Breathe.

SOPHIE: Don't worry. You'll do fine.
Shhhhhhh.

Soft sounds of an avalanche. SOPHIE moves with it.

Most of the time – there's not much point in talking.

She dances.

THEA and DA TENZING walk on until they reach the dead body in the down suit and stare transfixed at it. GEORGES has joined them and sinks to his knees nearby, not looking, just exhausted. DA TENZING takes off THEA's mask.

DA TENZING: Camp 2. This.

THEA: This.
Corpse.

GEORGES sees corpse and is overcome.

DA TENZING: Go to the tent and lie down.

THEA does as she is told. GEORGES stays where he is.

Night is falling.

T: Climbing or lying, we grow old and…

SOPHIE: Die.

T: Sophie – trust me – we should be so lucky.

SOPHIE: Should I trust you?

T: I don't know. What do you think?

SOPHIE: Don't know. Don't care. I'm going to have fun.

Camp Two

T is sitting on MALLORY's cairn.

Night: DA TENZING and THEA are huddled in the second tent in full gear. GEORGES is outside in full down gear trying to phone SOPHIE. SOPHIE is nearby, watching him.

THEA: He really met Tenzing?

DA TENZING: Twice. The day of Tenzing's happiness, my father touched his arm.

He touches THEA's arm lightly.

THEA: That all he got? One day?

DA TENZING: One day of perfect happiness – that's much in one life.

THEA: You should party more.
    You married?

DA TENZING: Of course. I have a son.

THEA: A son?

DA TENZING: Of course.

THEA: Of course.

DA TENZING: And a daughter.

THEA: Sure – a daughter.

DA TENZING: ?

THEA: Daughters – backup file.

DA TENZING: I haven't seen her yet. She was born last month. This trip – my wife asked me not to come. She shouted. She cried. But we need the money. Three more years like this and I'll be rich. A house in Darjeeling or Kathmandu. Maybe a trip to America.

THEA: Hey – look me up. Promise?

DA TENZING: You and Alice.

THEA: Alice? But…

DA TENZING grins.

Hey – Mom – was that a joke? You make a joke?

They grin at each other.

Hey! You got me!
Must be the altitude.

She takes a photograph out of her pocket.

This comes everywhere with me.
That's me at five.
I don't show many people this.
I wasn't very cute as a kid.

DA TENZING stares at the photograph.

Always the Indian. Never the cowboy. That's Calvin.
It's hard to be a kid.

Takes photo back.

I can always see so many points of view, you know?
I carry peoples' stories the way you carry their gear.
You porter. Me reporter.
That's neat, Thea.
I'd really like to understand you. Write about you, you know?

She takes out her pen and notebook.

Only time I don't feel everyone's pulling my strings is
when I write or when I climb.
My fingers are numb.

DA TENZING: Show me.

He takes her hand.

Two are white. I have pills to help. And you must take
antibiotics for this cut. The body has no resistance.

GEORGES enters the tent.

THEA: Fuck the Eagle Sun.
I'm going to write a book instead. My own expedition.
How I lost two fingers to the mountain. Personal detail.

GEORGES: Just how much – personal detail?

THEA: Who knows till the muse shows?
Hey – you should have thought of that before, Lom-bear,
you know?

He isn't amused.

What, Georges?

GEORGES: Sophie isn't picking up.

THEA: Maybe she's in bed with her lover.

GEORGES: Not amusing Thea. She had a hospital
appointment when I left.

THEA: She did? You left all the same.

GEORGES: She said I must. That's Sophie.

THEA: Oh, my sainted wife.

Bristling silence.

Gee, Georges. Our first almost argument. Give us time.
We could fight like leopards.

GEORGES: (*To DA TENZING.*) Are you going to the other tent?

DA TENZING moves, THEA stops him.

THEA: No. Too cold.
Let's all stay together tonight. I get to sleep in the middle.

She snuggles down. DA TENZING and GEORGES regard each other. DA TENZING lies down. GEORGES leaves the tent.

T: Did you say he must?

SOPHIE: Maybe.

T: Why?

SOPHIE: Oh – you know – men must work and women must weep.

Replay of SOPHIE and GEORGES' farewell:

You must go darling.

T: (*As GEORGES.*) Are you sure?

SOPHIE: Am I sure?

T: (*As GEORGES.*) Are you sure?

SOPHIE: Yes.

T: (*As GEORGES.*) Yes?

SOPHIE: Well – no.

T: (*As GEORGES.*) No?

SOPHIE: No. Not this time Georges. Is what I should have said. Fuck your training. And mine. I'm sick, Georges. I'm sick. Stay with me. Hold my hand. Be there.

GEORGES goes to the down body. Presently, THEA goes out to him.

GEORGES: (*Softly.*) I get restless.
Restless if I don't go.
She was sad, but she never said 'cancel'. Not even this
year. I offered.
I have to say I was relieved when she said 'go'.

SOPHIE: Go then. If you go – if you leave me like this –
don't come back. That's what I should have said.

T: Why didn't you?

SOPHIE: He might have not come back.

GEORGES: Six years getting ready for this. Six. And
suddenly: not going? Not getting to the top?
It's not the money.

SOPHIE: Me or the mountain Georges. Me or the mountain.
I should have said. Only it wasn't just the mountain. It
was her too. Something about her's made him reckless.
All the other ones he didn't make me know about. This
one scares me.

GEORGES: Imponderable, life. The alternatives;
mathematically. Doesn't pay ever, ever, to say: 'what
if', or 'I regret', or 'sorry'. We agreed.
We do as we do. Are as we are. Can't control outcomes.
Can't be responsible for each other. How can we?

SOPHIE: /Don't leave me alone.

GEORGES: /In the end, we're alone.

THEA: Are you really worried about her?

GEORGES: I knew when I left it could be serious. I'm a
shit. I shouldn't have come. But the mountain. You.
I couldn't not come. Travelling – being with you –
makes me feel so alive.

THEA: Georges? Can I hold you? I feel sad too, y' know,
sometimes.

GEORGES: Thank you. I'd rather be alone.

THEA: Sure.

She goes, then hesitates.

I've never seen you like this.

GEORGES: You'll soon learn to know me in all my moods.

THEA: Yeh? Maybe. Maybe not. I may not have the time between assignments.

GEORGES: I thought you liked commitment.

THEA: Did you.

GEORGES: You wrote about it all the time.

THEA: I write about a lot of things all the time, Georges. I like words, remember? It's what I do. I discuss commitment, I play with its configurations, I don't understand it. Except on a rock face.

GEORGES: It's why I took the risk to be here. When Sophie…

THEA: Ah: the storyline matures.

GEORGES: This isn't an assignment Thea. Or a pitch.

THEA: No? Georges – listen: my work's all I have that's me, you know? It's why you liked me in the first place.

GEORGES: I love you. Whatever work you do. It's you I love.

THEA: Until the day comes you suddenly change. Get sick of sponsoring me – then I need my pay check. And I'm good at what I do.

GEORGES: Your editor doesn't always agree.

THEA: Oh shit. Oh great. Action replay.
I've been here before.
Know what Georges? You're not making me laugh any
more.

She goes back to the tent.

He goes to the other tent to lie down.

DA TENZING: Georges is angry with me.

THEA: Me too.

DA TENZING: You're angry with me?

THEA: Georges is angry with me too.

DA TENZING: Why?

THEA: We don't like it when it gets real.

DA TENZING: You aren't real other times?

THEA: We try not to be. Lovers.

DA TENZING: Why?

THEA: The minute we get real, the mirrors crash and we
slash each other to ribbons. I know the type. Why Thea?
'Cos I'm the type.

DA TENZING: Why are you…

THEA: Lovers? I love him. Oh sure. I love everyone. So
long as they stay outside my story. It's the American
Way. Awshucks – Da T– I even love you too.

They lie down together.

T: And there it is: language. Language. 'Language' as my
mother used to say. 'Robin! Language!' Fuck me if it
doesn't impose on our brains the notion of straight lines,
of the necessity of a doer and someone done unto for
something to have been really, truly done: picking a

straw out of a whole field of hay, and basing on that one little Attic line the structure of Englishness, of Empire, of life itself and art and all its meaning.

The ark flounders on and linear on, as Aristotle told us it should, endlessly passing the port to our left, looking to shipwreck on Ararat and start a new life with God's blessing.

Is there no other way to map our lives?

I mean – look at Chinese. Pictures. Little cartoons, little rice seeds sprouting all ways in watery ground. Isn't this – doesn't this have to imply – a broader view of life's possibilities?

So – in the end we give our Empire back, rearranging our clothes, and China comes along and fucks Tibet.

Where be your ideograms now, you may say? Your Tao? Your ancient wisdom?

Fair point.

But we don't talk politics on expeditions.

Mountains have ears.

SOPHIE: Aristotle. Didn't he make up rules for telling stories?

This is my dream. What does a Greek man – a Greek *dead* man – a Greek dead *man* – know about the structure of an Englishwoman's dreams?

T: He said the sun circled the earth.

SOPHIE: Now that I understand.

T takes his camera off the tripod and packs it away.

T: We rage round the world and measure it. Draw up the rules for it. Frame it. Fix it. Conquer it. Label it. Knock it off, the bastard. Map the farthest point of what we desperately need to feel is solid earth.

And exactly what point is that?

How can a sphere of incomparable complexity, diversity, perversity, have points?

We measure our globe as we measure ourselves – plot it – grid it – draw and quarter it – slit it up the belly and lay it out like an orange skin, distorted, then point to a place and say: there – this is my peak – my pole – this is where I will find immortality for this thing I am – even if I don't know what this thing I am is – for life has to be a story with a beginning, middle and end, or all our momentary lapses of courage – here, now – would send us mad. No?

So: this will be my goal, the meaning of my life – my Happy Ever After.

My Ever-Rest.

But she flows.

I change.

Will I change again?

From the cairn, T pockets MALLORY's goggles.

The Lhotse Face

Stupa stage four: air/green.

DA TENZING Exits the tent first and goes to the down body.

DA TENZING: (*Ignoring T.*) The second time my father sees Tenzing is in Darjeeling. Still he floats above the earth. Still, like a god. More like a god than ever, only this time, more like Kali – old men often look like women. His face is white. Cheekbones like her mountain ridges. It rains all day. Early monsoon – or late – I don't remember what my father says. The white *khatas* – so many – cling to his body and round his neck; the marigolds wash from his hands. They wait and wait for the rain to stop and in the end, his son Norbu pours ghee on the pyre and it bursts into flames with a great roar – like an avalanche. An avalanche of red. After that there's no sound but the rain and the hissing, until his skull cracks.

Sound of ice cracking. It begins to snow.

Pause.

They say his lungs collapsed. They say his liver shrank to the size of a dried leaf. They say he died unhappy. So he must have left his smiles on the slopes of Chomolungma. He will find them again when he returns.
We go on.

He goes to light the stove.

SOPHIE goes to the down body and takes its gear to put on.

T: 'Clothes are a perishable second grave for the loved one.'

SOPHIE: What?

T: I say things like that.

SOPHIE: I've decided not to mind.

She goes to the fixed rope.

(*To DA TENZING.*) Excuse me.

DA TENZING: ?

SOPHIE: How do I…?

DA TENZING: You use this.

He gives her a jumar clip.

You jumar.

He mimes jumar-ing then goes back to preparing food.

SOPHIE: Thank you so much.

She is mystified. THEA emerges from the tent and regards SOPHIE with interest.

I've never climbed before.

THEA: Lady – you've got this far. Not that this is climbing. This is yak stuff.

SOPHIE: Is it? Yaks do this?

THEA: Yeh.

SOPHIE: Who'd've believed it?
    What's climbing then if it isn't just going up?

THEA: Ma'am…
    OK.

She gets rid of the jumar. Light changes to subtle green as she takes off her down and strips to her indoor climbing gear. She ropes SOPHIE for a real climb.

Go on – shoot up.

SOPHIE: Me? I don't do heights.

THEA: Once in your life!
    Take a trip you don't control!

She talks her up the climb.

SOPHIE makes the top. Great jubilation.

SOPHIE: Aren't you coming too?

THEA: Me? Sure.
    (*To DA TENZING.*) Hey Mom – keep breakfast warm.

She starts to follow and freezes on the vertical face.

GEORGES exits shivering from his tent.

GEORGES: What's that?

DA TENZING: Corsani. For the potatoes. Chilli. Garlic. Salt.

GEORGES: Potatoes and – ?

DA TENZING: Corsani.

GEORGES: Where's Thea?

DA TENZING gestures.

Good night?

No response.

What are you thinking?

DA TENZING: Nothing.

GEORGES: What do you think when we walk?

DA TENZING is silent. GEORGES is furious.

How can you think nothing?

DA TENZING hands him a plate. DA TENZING eats.

Like a shadow aren't you?
Always at my ankles – never something to get hold of.
Or detach.

DA TENZING: Snow…

GEORGES: ?

DA TENZING: I think – snow – setting round my mouth. And demons – Demons – all around us.

GEORGES: You think?

DA TENZING: I see.

GEORGES: Good or bad?

DA TENZING shrugs.

Are they always here – or climbing with us?

DA TENZING: How do I know? I'm only here when I'm here.

GEORGES: And they're here now? You see them?

DA TENZING nods.

Aren't you afraid?

DA TENZING: What can I do? I trust them. That's all I can do. And my job.

He eats.

You OK? You should eat. Feeling sick?

GEORGES nods and shivers.

Want anything? Water?

GEORGES nods. DA TENZING helps him to water.

Head OK? Aspirin?

GEORGES: Oxygen I think. Please.

DA TENZING goes to fetch a mask and GEORGES puts it on.

Thea's Dream

Air turns greener.

THEA is poised on the face. SOPHIE is watching her from above.

THEA: You ask a question with your body – with all your
body. All your body goes '?' And the rock curls into the
mark. Like a lover curls into your body to sleep.
The questions get better as the body learns to move over
the rock. Like lovemaking gets better the more ways you
try it – the more lovers you have.
There are always more questions to ask and more rock
to twist the answers. And soon neither the questions nor
the answers matter as much as the climb.
The climb you can't stop making.
The climb you can't stop making.
The climb you can't stop making.

She climbs.

I fell off the face of the Old Man of the Mountains once.
Franconia. I just hung upside down swinging on the rope,
laughing.

She hangs by her foot from the rope.

83

Flying.

When I get back to school, the editor of the school paper asks me to write it up: my first press assignment.

So, OK: the mountain's interviewing me, OK? Flying upside down in front of him.

Ghost of OLD MAN of the mountains appears (SOPHIE).

OLD MAN: (*SOPHIE.*) What the fuck you swinging there for, Thea?

THEA: You are one ugly old geek – thought you might look better upside down.

OLD MAN: You scared?

She rights herself on the rope.

THEA: What of?

OLD MAN: Me: sawing this rope with my teeth and letting you fall.

THEA: Try it. I'll flip. Calvin has his cape and tight little blue pants. He'll streak up here one hand like this (*Superman pose*), tuck me under his arm and fly twice round the world with me. So: Fuck you, Old Man. I'm Me-A!

She slips.

OLD MAN: Just like all the other girls. Can't deliver.

He laughs.

THEA: Watch me Mom. I'm good.

She climbs, shouting.

Me-a!

ECHO: Meameameameameameameameamea…

GHOST OF THEA'S EDITOR: Thea? It's Doug. Remember me sweetheart? Your employer? Babe – it's still all over the map. Where's the focus? I know there's not a lot of air there, but you're redefining breathless prose. What gives?

THEA: (*To OLD MAN/SOPHIE.*) You were supposed to read my report before he saw it.

GHOST OF THEA'S EDITOR: The tenth graf – that whole bit about the purity of snow and angels – I mean, sure I've read the metaphysicals, but Alice Dodge in Providence – nah – NOT! Get real, Thea. Comes from nowhere, goes the same way. Find a context for it, please?

OLD MAN: Get your Mom to sign, so we know it's all your own work.

THEA: What's the shithead mean, all my own work? How do I know if it's all my own work? Have to put concrete in my ears and tape down my eyelids not to be beholden to someone. Something.
God knows I try to do it on my own. Without you.

She starts to climb up to OLD MAN/SOPHIE: freezes again.

Georges' Dream

The air is still green, like mustard gas. The wind is getting stronger. Distant sounds of avalanche like guns on the battlefield.

GEORGES crawls to the down body.

Ghosts including ENKIDU (DA TENZING) appear.

GEORGES: I watch the operation from so far away. Over oceans. The body has no face. No head. The blade's in my hand. Slicing through huge crevasses, digging in the white flesh. Keeping my skill constant and essential, I slip the blade through, never touching ligament or tendon. Let alone bone.

He gives a little cry.

The chest is empty.
I can't find the heart.

Pause.

I see threads of grey cells creeping like a slow land slip, like lava before the air torches it. The head lifts up. It was only hidden – a white sheet. The eyes are open. Looking into mine.
(*Whispers.*) Sophie…
I turn away. In my dream. I walk. I walk. I walk. I walk. I walk. Away. Always. Away.
But the ground's tipping up and up, growing, rising, curling over my head, and – the mountain, the mountain falls on me. Strikes my temple. Tears my feet from under me. I'm buried. Still breathing: rocks wedged in my lung cavities, my heart beating fast – too fast – I'm falling in darkness. Arresting. Falling. But – inside myself. Falling inside – and the fall has no end. I dig my fingers into the scree. I hear the bones in my legs and ribs snapping. I feel my clothes and skin tearing into ribbons and birds screaming and blood pouring out my mouth and ears.
Never been so afraid. Never been so alone. Someone. Hold my hand!

The wind rises.

Someone's there…

ENKIDU: (*DA TENZING.*) Now you see, my friend. Ghosts everywhere. Sitting in darkness, dust on their white lips, clay stuck to their teeth, hugging arms like bird's wings around themselves against the battering cold wind. And always, she is there…

YETI appears (*SOPHIE/OLD MAN*) (*'A white human bird with lion's feet and eagle's claws for hands'* – ed.)

…she tears our hair and rips our clothes and pinions our arms and shreds the flesh to plant the quills of feathers in the streams of blood.

GEORGES: …I look up and see the white flesh and stone green eyes of…

Terrible cry, birdlike, monstrous:

YA-TE: (*SOPHIE/OLD MAN.*) Irkalla, Queen of Darkness/ Ereshkigal, Queen of Death!

GEORGES screams.

YETI and ENKIDU disappear.

T approaches to find DA TENZING nursing GEORGES.

GEORGES: Help me.

T: (*To DA TENZING.*) Maybe he should turn round?

DA TENZING: I've warned him.
He's the boss.

GEORGES: I'm fine. Fine. I'll get there. She's… (*Broken.*) Thea…I can't…Jesus.
I'm so afraid.

DA TENZING: Keep him warm.

They put him in a sleeping bag. T goes over to the body of clothes.

T: 'Emperor Yao went to see the four masters in the distant Ku-She Mountains, and when he returned north of the Fen River deep in thought, he found he'd given up all beneath heaven in those mountains.'
Do you know this one?

DA TENZING shrugs.

Sherpa.

DA TENZING: *Sherpani.* They die, too, the women now.
    All over the mountain.

T: That makes you angry.

DA TENZING: No. It just is.
    He's not so good.
    Will you keep an eye on him?
    I must follow Thea.

T nods and crouches by the body.

DA TENZING puts his mask on and follows THEA.

*GEORGES gets out of his bag and crouches across the body
from T.*

GEORGES: Me. Some day. Soon.

T: Mmmmm.

GEORGES: One day. You.

T: Ah – sadly –

They stare at each other.

Yes?

GEORGES: You don't –
    I don't want –
    My life –

Pause.

She is so. Beautiful. So. Hard to…

Pause.

Her mouth –

SOPHIE has come down to them.

T: Beautiful. Yes.

GEORGES: Could you advise me?

T: About?

GEORGES: My life.

T: What's wrong with it?

GEORGES: I love Sophie. I worry about her. I need her. / But…

SOPHIE: / But…

Pause.

GEORGES: I keep thinking about the mountain, you know? Mountains. So white. So pure. So –

T: Yes?

Sound of an avalanche.

GEORGES: I'm Swiss.

T: Neutral, yes.

GEORGES: We know something about mountains.
Something you English never dream: hollow. Filled with darkness.
You think I'm mad. That my brain is sick. I've seen it. Swiss, you see.
Bunkers under the Alps. The army – is – inside. Waiting. Swiss join their army for life. Men. We can never leave the army.
The future: every Swiss – guaranteed survival. The only country with enough food, enough shelter – every man, woman and child. Not a dream for us: Armageddon.
And afterwards – ours will be the only country left.

T: Running like clockwork.

GEORGES: I left all that behind.
No more shadows.
I love life.

T: So what's wrong?

GEORGES looks round, afraid.

GEORGES: Demons. Demons. Climbing with me. He said so. He saw them. That's why the snow slides.
I'm scared. There's something wrong with my heart.

SOPHIE: It needs a Lambert valve.

She hoots with laughter. GEORGES is unaware of her. She sobers up.

Poor Georges.

T: I just take photographs – why ask me? I take them because I can't bear to lose the present. Then in the future I can't bear to look at them and remember what's past. In trying to catch the moment – I lose it forever.
Takes courage to leap.
And to compromise.
I do neither.
Want my advice, Georges? Go home. Eat. Drink. Dance. Be happy. Wash your clothes. Have a bath. Love the little child that holds your hand. Make your wife smile. Before it's too late.

Long pause. Sounds of choughs calling.

GEORGES: I have a son of thirty one who hasn't spoken to me for twenty years. I love Sophie, god knows. But right now I want…

T: /Thea.

GEORGES: /to make the top.

T: Go on then. Go up.

GEORGES: How can I? I might die!

T: You want the dream of another life. A new life. On top of the world. Don't you?

GEORGES: There are too many dreams to follow in the world, too many paths I want to try…

T: Trouble is, my friend – in my experience – you have to die this time. Are you willing? To die, Georges? Are you prepared to take that risk?

GEORGES: My heart… (*He feels it.*) Should it be doing this?

T: For a little time. A little time. Recovery's always round the corner. One way or another. Fast and sure. Hold on.

GEORGES: I don't want to die. Help me. I want to lead a good life. What shall I do?

T: Oh. They'll tell you all sorts of things when you get home. The pundits.
But it's simple. You'll be surprised how simple it is.
You only have to stay awake. Just stay awake, Georges.
That's all.

Thea's Dream. Reprise

THEA is alone on the face. The light is green. The wind blows fiercely. Mist. She slips. She slips again. Thea appears stuck on the wall.

THEA: Help me. Someone?

OLD MAN: What now?

THEA: Can't move.

OLD MAN: Where's your guts Thea?

THEA: Not me.
Not afraid.

OLD MAN: No? What then?

THEA: Can't move.

OLD MAN: Go home. And Thea – shave your armpits if you're gonna wear Lycra.

THEA: Fuck you.

OLD MAN: Like all women. Want it both ways.

THEA: Hedy Lamarr got a patent for torpedoes and the mobile phone.

OLD MAN: Hedy Lamarr turned down Casablanca, sweetheart.

THEA: Smart bitch. Casablanca sucks!

OLD MAN: And now she's got an unattended death. Just like this one, Thea.

THEA: Please –

OLD MAN: Chicken. Can't collect. Can't deliver. Can't move. Can't write. Can't love. Can't live.

THEA: No!

OLD MAN: Hey, here's a two-line head:
'Eagle chick flies against the ice.
And flattens herself dead.'
What's the matter? You can climb, you say. You always want to climb. So: climb.

ECHO: Climbclimbclimbclimbclimbclimbclimbclimb…

THEA: Calvin!

No echo.

Help me!

OLD MAN: Don't hang on. That's how you die. Use your friend. All these years: doncha learn nothing?

THEA: Help me. Someone.

She starts to cry.

OLD MAN: Chicken.

THEA: It's perfect. I climb faults. If it's perfect, you can't go anywhere. If it turns perfect, it's over.
Nowhere to stick the friend.

She struggles to bolt into the wall. Green light becomes very bright.

GHOST OF THEA'S EDITOR: Thea? You on line? Too much descriptive stuff about the people. Remember quotes darling? Use them, lots of them. And shorter sentences. And that Tenzing clone – the Sherpa – I mean, you drone on with all this crypto-biographic, spiritual crap, but do we ever get to know the guy? So far, he's a ghost. Can you make him real for me? Thea?

THEA falls.

Lights cut.

Otherwise it's fine. Keep it coming.

Dance: the Death Zone

GEORGES is lying, THEA is falling, DA TENZING is flying. SOPHIE and T are at the centre of the movement.

GEORGES: See: if you…

THEA: See: if you…

DA TENZING: See: if you…

GEORGES: Get too honest it all gets confused. Women and men. It seems natural to me there should be lovers. Not that I'm promiscuous. I'm always very careful.
I only fall in love once or twice, and even then I soon come to my senses. Never need to hold on. Never need to need. I build bridges. I move on. The bridges fall behind me.
If I'd known – would I have come?
It hurts. It hurts. It tears me. This half of me is numb.

Dead.
Never mind.
If I can get home – it can't be damaged.
Can it.
I'm so cold.

Pause.

Sometimes I dream she's lying with me.

THEA: Miss someone too much it all gets confused. Women and men. Am I afraid of falling?
Yes – in an excited sort of way.
Falling's free. It may or may not be a choice, but it's free.
I think I will fall, one day.
I think I think I will. Who knows though, if we really think we will?
I sort of look forward to it. My life started that day
I climbed and it finishes the day I fall. As long as a piece of rope without a knot: my life. It stops at the end, suddenly. And I think I think that's fine.
Cross my heart and hope to die.

Pause.

Sometimes I dream he's falling with me.

DA TENZING: Talk too much it all gets confused. Women and men. I dream of standing alone on the summit of Chomolungma, scratching in the snow, and finding chocolate and lollies and biscuits, and laughing and hearing my laughter echoing around all the white valleys of the world. Then I see her again.
And I fly, then, lifted by the wind of my laughter.
I wheel over the rolling mountains – they are so small beneath me. A huge figure stands on the summit of the world, smiling at me: is it Siva? Or Kali? I look for Tenzing. I am Tenzing. I have four lungs, and two mouths. No one knows what this means.

Pause.

Sometimes I dream she's flying with me.

They bring their head torches together to beam light on T.

T: Turn around time.
Most climbers die on the way down. Survival can depend
on the will of the person in question entirely. Seaborne
Beck Weathers on the Geneva Spur listened to his pundit,
waited too long in the storm of '96 and nearly died. But
his will – was mountainous. Apparently – one key
question is – do you have anything to go back for?

THEA and GEORGES are packing up.

THEA: I remember an old man, tapping his way with a
stick across my beach. Says hello. I say hi back. Later he
trips. I see him lying there. Feel like maybe I trampled a
chick, and crunched his bones, saying hi back.
That was the year Calvin goes out in Dad's car and
doesn't come back. No reason. Says bye, Sis! Then dies.
Just driving.
Always think things are my fucking fault.
Always feel, wherever I put my feet, I send avalanches
onto peoples' heads.

T: Sometimes it pays to shut our eyes. Just shut your eyes,
sometimes, Thea.

THEA: No one ever tells me why he died. He's old. I think
that's it. Time to fall. That's why. The ocean sweeps his
stick away.
He'll be my first story.
I'm going to write it up.

She goes to GEORGES and kisses him.

GEORGES: Will I see you again?

THEA: Whenever you have a mountain to climb – I'll be
there. Call me. Please.

She goes to T.

I really love Georges you know. Beneath that mirrorglass exterior beats…

T: …a heart of gold.

THEA: I wish I could take you back with me to see New York.

T: Thea –

THEA: I know. I know.
Bye.

She kisses T and leaves.

GEORGES: Imponderable. Life. The alternatives; mathematically. Doesn't pay ever, ever, to say: 'what if', or 'I regret', or 'sorry'. We agreed.
We do as we do. Are as we are. Can't control outcomes. Can't be responsible for each other. How can we? In the end, we're alone.
I'm going home for Sophie.

He leaves.

Sophie's Story Ends

During this speech, SOPHIE returns to her hospital.

SOPHIE: I told him: there's no going back until after the tunnel. He drove a little way further, digesting this piece of unwelcome information, then stopped the car on the hard shoulder in the middle where the stone wall had a gap and a chain, leaped out, unhooked the chain and U-turned into the fast lane of the oncoming traffic. Had there been any oncoming traffic. Which, as I say, rather spookily, there was, by now, not. Not one car. Not a sign of life.
No sound on the motorway but the purr of the hired engine and the soft metallic chunk of the chain, relocating.

And then our laughter.
I remember our laughter so, so much more than anything else.
Like naughty children breaking rules – which is what we were, really. Hoping for the grown-up to swoop down and punish us, save us from our own joy. Still finding it hard not to find someone to ask permission to be wild, and laugh.
Never dreaming it might be ourselves we needed to ask. Not then.
Then another thing arrests me: where are the cars? Where is everybody? Has the world ended somehow beyond Aosta and we've missed it? A meteorite in Arizona?
A sudden and cataclysmic atomic war between India and Pakistan? Armageddon from one single decisive addition to the ozone layer via our exhaust pipe finally cutting off the world's oxygen supply, and me, in a Fiat oxygen bubble – the last survivor? But no – he's outside dancing in front of the windscreen.

A ghost dances in front of her.

Not drowning, but dancing.
No signs of suffocation. Nor of running away. He comes back. He grins at me.
His grin…

Pause. She grins back. Then stops.

Then I remember:
The Mont Blanc Tunnel's closed. *That's* why no cars. The fire a few weeks before. Forty dead. Twisted metal, fused rock and ghosts. Death's at the heart of the mountain creeping back along the concrete artery towards us, like mustard gas in Flanders trenches.
But he breaks the rules. U-turns. Grins.
Swiss, you see. Not English.

Pause. Smiles.

I am perfectly, utterly – happy.

GEORGES arrives with flowers and takes SOPHIE's hand.

Poor Georges.
I'll be dead soon.
So will you.

GEORGES: We'll get a second opinion.

T: The ark runs aground. The cask snaps open. The beasts are loose on the mountain.

A Dream of Beasts

GEORGES and SOPHIE speak simultaneously.

THE SNAKE: (*GEORGES.*) /A curious sensation…as if we drifted near the edge of a field with a wall at the edge – a low wall, somehow unbreachable. The field, I remember, was a bright and uniform green, like flood water, and we were sailing towards the edge, and a sign said: 'Thus far and no further'.

THE YETI: (*SOPHIE.*) /I lost my wedding ring. Threw it away. I see as I go higher it doesn't matter really – there's a yellow band around the mountain, studded with fish spines. They crumble under my feet as I climb the last few feet. I've come up too high on my own. It's alright though. If I get through this, he'll be there, waiting: up with the gold.

DA TENZING and THEA fly over the mountain together, land and dig for chocolates and lollies and biscuits, and find them.

DA TENZING also finds MALLORY's film.

She teases him as though he were CALVIN, he loves her as though she were NIMA.

DA TENZING and THEA speak simultaneously.

THE GORAK: (*THEA.*) / When I looked down I saw Valle Paradiso. There was the stone I remember, lying in the valley with lichens on – orange. It glowed like gold in the sun, and I can see the shape if I close my eyes.

She closes her eyes.

Two shapes: a bird, with wings out stiff like a plane, flying towards a sun. Her beak holds something. She is almost touching the sun. An eagle of gold. A Westerly Sun.

THE YAK: (*DA TENZING.*) / My father says: a *sharwar* boy looks up and sees a mountain. He looks down and what does he see? A load. He picks up the load and starts for the mountain. This load is not a burden to be struggled with and cursed at. It is part of his body. They are all part of my body.

He shrugs.

Thuji Chey, Chomolungma.
I am grateful.

It begins to snow.

T: Every snowflake slots with the precision of technology: binding, waiting, bridging, loosing, burying.

Sound of avalanche.

We walk always beneath the benediction of avalanches.

Goes to the cairn.

You wish you had your camera, too, don't you?

Rolls the stones away and scatters the memorials.

The wealth of nations and the cream of climbers comb the flanks of the Mother Goddess of the Snows like she's Clapham Common after a particularly nasty murder.

They frisk corpses known and unknown, trawl through rubbish heaps and risk death and the mountain's rage. For what? For this.

He produces the Kodak VP camera from his breast pocket.

Or one very much like it.
Why?
Don't know why.

Grins.

Know where.
Are we alone? Or together?
I'm beside myself.

Grins.

'Waiting for my soul to catch up.'
What's a life?
I've had three.
Man. Woman. Leopard.
Not necessarily the best way of putting it.
Three – at least.
Three – speaking in terms of models.
Three: a body containing space. Like a tent. Like a woman. Like a mountain. Like a camera.
Let's see.

He opens the camera.

Empty.
That's it, then.
Beached.
Always wanted to know what it would feel like to be cut off by the tide.

T strips and lies down over the outline of MALLORY.

Darkness falls.

Summit Day

Stupa stage 5/1: light.

Ghosts gather around T.

DA TENZING enters wearing a head torch, carrying one for T, and warm clothes to dress him in.

DA TENZING: I wish the yeti would eat you and your
    camera.

T: What are you doing up here?
    The others are gone.
    It's finished.

DA TENZING: I come to find you, before she eats you.

T: Why?

DA TENZING: It's what's in here kills you, not she.

He touches T.

    Cold.
    How long you been up here?

T: That's the question. I'm waiting. That's the answer.
    To another question.

DA TENZING: Go. Move. Warm up.

T: I'll try.

DA TENZING: Of course. We try. Try for a while. Until
    Ya-te comes for us, you try.

He pulls a sweet out of his pocket.

    Have a sweet. (*Grins.*) I found them. *Tondai.* Suck. Energy.

They sit and suck on a sweet.

    Where's your goggles?
    What a ramshackly man you are.

T: We've had this conversation.

DA TENZING: It'll be dark soon.

T: It's dark already.

DA TENZING waves his hand in front of T's face.

DA TENZING: You blind? Snow blind.

He feels in T's discarded jacket for MALLORY's goggles. Pulls out the unpaid bill.

What a man you are. Unpaid bills on Everest.

T: Gamages will mount a rescue.

DA TENZING finds the goggles and tries to put them on T.

Don't trouble, dear boy.
I've always been blind.

DA TENZING: Blind? How did you get this far?

T: One should never be too busy to play Fives.

DA TENZING looks at the sky and pulls a vivid white hood over his head.

DA TENZING: You say. When you want to move, old boy.

He lies down.

Stupid man. Stupid foreigners.

T: (*Tenderly.*) A Sherpa sleeps all night once on
Chomolungma – and lives…

Ghosts gather.

DA TENZING: So many times she asked me not to go to
this mountain.
Now I don't have to go again.

T: She'll be missing you. Worried.

DA TENZING: Every night until the day she dies she lights a candle. In case I ever find my way home.

Ghost of TENZING'S MOTHER appears

GHOST OF TENZING'S MOTHER: (*SOPHIE.*) Did you see the beasts my son?

DA TENZING: Yes mother.

GHOST OF TENZING'S MOTHER: Proof! (*Whispering.*) And *did* you see Kali and Siva…?

Ghosts of KALI and SIVA (THEA and GEORGES.) appear and embrace.

DA TENZING: Embracing, yes. Sacred marriage: *Ru.*

GHOST OF TENZING'S MOTHER: *Namas-te*!

ECHO: (*Ghosts.*)
Namastenamastenamastenamastenamastenamaste

DA TENZING: I found something else. Look.

He shows the film from MALLORY's camera.

T: On the summit?

DA TENZING: Let's see what's on it.

T: Why? We know the answer now. Mallory's left us a sign.

DA TENZING: Let's see what's on it.

DA TENZING gets up suddenly and puts T's head torch on for him – (Gives him his third eye.)

T: What are you doing?

DA TENZING: Guiding. Stupid man.
This is the time to do it. We do it or die.
Do it and die. Can't do it alone.
Be great. Make others great. That's what she says –

Chomolungma.
Climb. Not as a soldier to an enemy, but with love, as a child climbs on the lap of its mother: climb.

The thaw begins.

Listen:
The thaw begins.

An avalanche is threatening.

T climbs the mountain – the ghosts hold it steady for him.

DA TENZING: *Ça va bien*!

T: She's a wave, Everest. Slow down and see her breaking.

Sound of an avalanche grows.

DA TENZING: What do you see?

Avalanche grows.

T: (*Delighted.*) Nothing! I see nothing!

GHOSTS/DA TENZING: What do you see?
Who got there first?
Who got there first?
Who got there first? etc.

The avalanche crashes over the scene: a white party tent with rainbow lights, over everyone including audience.

Tibetan rainbow death: T disappears into light leaving only his heart (the red pouch) his tongue (the red scarf) and his eyes (goggles? camera? head torch?)

From the dark room a projector beams out into the space showing slides in front of the summit backdrop from MALLORY's camera; first the shots taken at the beginning of the play – audience – theatre staff – children – everyone – rolling on and on.

The End.